D0263078

Please return/renew this item by the last date shown

worcestershire
countycouncil
Libraries & Learning

André Comte-Sponville is one of France's pre-eminent contemporary philosophers. Previously a professor at the Sorbonne, he is the author of *A Short Treatise on the Great Virtues*, an international bestseller that has been translated into twenty-five languages. He lives in Paris.

The Book of
Atheist Spirituality

André Comte-Sponville

Translated by Nancy Huston

BANTAM BOOKS

LONDON • TORONTO • SYDNEY • AUCKLAND • JOHANNESBURG

TRANSWORLD PUBLISHERS
61–63 Uxbridge Road, London W5 5SA
A Random House Group Company
www.rbooks.co.uk

**THE BOOK OF ATHEIST SPIRITUALITY
A BANTAM BOOK: 9780553819908**

First published in Great Britain
in 2008 by Bantam Press
a division of Transworld Publishers
Bantam edition published 2009

A CIP catalogue record for this book
is available from the British Library.

Addresses for Random House Group Ltd companies outside the UK
can be found at: www.randomhouse.co.uk
The Random House Group Ltd Reg. No. 954009

The Random House Group Limited supports The Forest Stewardship Council (FSC),
the leading international forest certification organisation. All our titles that are
printed on Greenpeace approved FSC certified paper carry the FSC logo. Our
paper procurement policy can be found at www.rbooks.co.uk/environment

Typeset in A Caslon
Printed in the UK by CPI Cox & Wyman, Reading, RG1 8EX.

2 4 6 8 10 9 7 5 3 1

This book is dedicated to
the woman who brought it forth

Contents

Introduction

Over the past few years, the revival of religion has taken on spectacular and, in many ways, frightening dimensions. This is clearly the case in Muslim countries, but everything seems to indicate that the Western world, though in a different way, is equally affected by the phenomenon. Is it a revival of spirituality? If it were, we could only welcome it with open arms. Is it a revival of faith? That wouldn't be a problem either. Unfortunately, it is all too often accompanied by dogmatism, obscurantism, fundamentalism – and sometimes fanaticism. It would be a mistake to leave the field to these forces. The struggle for enlightenment continues; never has it been more urgent, and it is a struggle for freedom.

Is it a struggle against religion? No; rather, it is a struggle in favour of tolerance, in favour of the separation of church and state, in favour of the freedom to believe or not believe. The spirit is no one's private property, nor is freedom.

I was raised a Christian. My feelings about this are neither bitter nor angry – quite the opposite. I owe much of what I am, or what I try to be, to the Christian religion, and therefore to the Christian (in my case Catholic) church. My morality has scarcely changed at all since my pious years. Nor has my sensitivity. Even my way of being an atheist bears the imprint of the faith to which I subscribed throughout my childhood and adolescence. This is nothing to be ashamed of or even surprised at. It is part of my history – or, rather, it is part of *our* history. What would the Western world be without Christianity? What would the world itself be without both? Being an atheist by no means entails being amnesiac. Humanity is one; both religion and irreligion are part of it; neither are sufficient unto themselves.

I loathe obscurantism, fanaticism and superstition. I find nihilism and servility equally repellent. Spirituality is far too important a matter to be left to fundamentalists. Tolerance is far too precious a possession to be confused with indifference or laxity. Nothing could be worse than letting ourselves be deadlocked into a confrontation between the fanaticism of some – no matter what religion they lay claim to – and the nihilism of others. Far better to combat both, without either conflating them or falling into their respective traps.

The name of this combat is the separation of church and state. It remains for atheists to invent the spirituality that goes with it. This is the task to which the present book hopes to contribute. I've deliberately made it brief and accessible – so as to get straight to the essentials and address the greatest possible number of readers. It seemed to me that the task at hand was an urgent one. Erudition and the quarrels of experts can wait; freedom of thought cannot.

What are 'the essentials'? In spiritual matters, it seemed to me that they could be summed up in three questions. Firstly, can we do without religion? Secondly, does God exist? And thirdly, can there be an atheist spirituality? This little book reflects my search for the answers to these questions. Atheists have as much spirit as everyone else; why would they be less interested in spiritual life?

Chapter I

Can We Do Without Religion?

Let us begin with the easiest part. God, by definition, surpasses us. Religions do not. They are human – all too human, some would say – and, as such, accessible to our understanding.

God, if he exists, is transcendent. Religions are part of history, society, the world (they are immanent).

God is reputed to be perfect. No religion can ever be so.

The existence of God is open to question (as will be discussed in the second chapter). The existence of religions is not. Thus, the questions raised by religions are not so much ontological as sociological or existential: we need to ask, not whether religions exist (unfortunately, they often seem to exist too much!), but what they are and whether we could do without them. It is especially the latter question that interests me, but in order to answer it we must first take at least a brief look at the former.

What Are Religions?

The notion of religion is so vast and various that it is not easy to find an adequate definition of it. What could shamanism and Buddhism, Taoism and Islam, Confucianism and Christianity possibly have in common? Might it be a mistake to use the same word, *religion*, for all these things? I sometimes think so. Several of these systems of belief, the Eastern ones in particular, seem to me to be a mixture of spirituality, ethics and philosophy rather than a *religion* in the generally accepted Western sense of the word. They are less about God than they are about human beings or nature. They have to do less with faith than with meditation; their practices are not so much rites and rituals as they are exercises and requirements; and their followers assemble not so much in churches as in schools of life or wisdom. This is especially true of Buddhism, Taoism and Confucianism, at least in their pure or purified forms – that is, independent of the superstitions that, in all countries, tend to accrete around a doctrine, sometimes to the point of making it unrecognizable. They are sometimes referred to as atheistic or agnostic religions. While the expression may sound self-contradictory to Western ears, it is far from absurd. Not only are Buddha, Lao-tzu and Confucius not gods themselves; they identify with no deity, no revelation, no personal or transcendent Creator of any sort. They are merely men of freedom, men who have been freed; wise men; spiritual guides.

But let us move on. I am neither an ethnologist nor a historian of religions. As a philosopher, I wonder about the possibility of leading a good life without religion. In order to answer this question, I need to know what religion is, and thus I must come up with a definition of the word, however approximate and temporary. One definition people often find enlightening is the one quoted by Émile Durkheim in the first chapter of his *Elementary Forms of Religious Life*: 'A religion is a solidary system of beliefs and practices relative to things sacred, that is to say, set apart and taboo – beliefs and practices which bring together those who adhere to them in a moral community known as a church.' Certain elements of this definition may be debatable – the sacred is not only taboo and set apart, it is also revered; the community of believers is not necessarily a church; and so forth – but not, I think, its general thrust. It will be noted that it makes no reference to one or several gods. That is because Durkheim knew that some religions had no gods – Jainism, for instance, which is atheistic, and Buddhism, which is 'an ethics without God and an atheism without Nature' (the phrase, quoted by Durkheim, is from the writings of Eugène Burnouf, the great nineteenth-century scholar of India). All theisms are religious, but not all religions are theistic.

Durkheim's definition, centred round the notions of the sacred and the community, gives us what we can call the broad sociological or ethnological meaning of the word *religion*. As I myself belong, for reasons of personal history, to a monotheistic universe, and more specifically to the field of Western philosophy, I would like to propose a more limited definition, one that is not so much ethnological as it is theological or metaphysical, one that can be seen as a subset of Durkheim's. In our parts of the world, a religion is almost always a belief in one or several deities. Were we to combine the two definitions, as vocabulary itself encourages us to do (but without conflating them), we could come up with the following formulation, a reiteration and extension of Durkheim's: by *religion*, we mean any organized set of beliefs and rituals involving the sacred, the supernatural or the transcendent (this is the broad sense of the term) and specifically involving one or several gods (this is the restricted sense), which beliefs and rituals unite those who recognize and practise them into a moral and spiritual community.

Was the original Buddhism a religion, in this sense of the word? I'm not certain that it was. Buddha asserted the existence of no deity, and it is doubtful that the words 'sacred', 'supernatural' or 'transcendent' would have meant much to him, or to his least superstitious followers. Yet it is clear that, historically speaking, Buddhism *became* a religion – with its temples, dogmas, rites and prayers, its sacred or purportedly supernatural objects. Much the same thing is true of Taoism and Confucianism. Such wisdom at the outset! So many superstitions over the centuries! Almost everywhere, the need to believe tends to win out over the desire for freedom.

The least that can be said is that the Western world is no exception to this rule. It, too, developed schools of thought imbued with great wisdom, but these were rapidly subsumed by the very religiosity that, for a while, they had purported to replace. Faith and reason – *mythos* and *logos* – coexist; this is what is known as civilization. Our own civilizations have been nourished on transcendence for centuries. How could they not bear the imprint of this nourishment? In our part of the world, animism and polytheism are no more. I don't feel nostalgic about their disappearance – on the contrary! It was a first step, as Max Weber has shown, towards the rationalization of reality. Nature has been emptied of its gods – nothing remains, as Alain once put it, but the emptiness of the desert and 'the formidable, all-present absence'. *That* is still very much alive. Judaism, Christianity and Islam are indeed religions, in the restricted sense of the word I have just delineated. And in our part of the world, it is these three monotheisms that matter the most.

Personal Testimony

Can we do without religion? Obviously, it all depends on what is meant by *we*. Who are *we*?

If *we* is a series of individuals, then I must say that I personally have no trouble at all living without religion!

I know what I'm talking about – or, at least, I can compare: not only was I raised a Christian, but I also believed in God. My faith, if occasionally laced with doubts, was powerful until around age eighteen. Then I lost it, and it felt like a liberation – everything suddenly seemed simpler, lighter, stronger and more open. It was as if I had left childhood behind me, with its fantasies and fears, its closeness and languorousness, and entered the real world at long last – the adult world, the world of action, the world of truth, unhampered by forgiveness or Providence. Such freedom! Such responsibility! Such joy! Yes, I'm convinced that my life has been better – more lucid, freer and more intense – since I became an atheist.

Of course, this does not necessarily apply to everyone. Many people who have converted would say just the opposite, namely, that they have led a better life since they became believers; and many believers, even if they've done nothing but share their parents' religion since childhood, would describe it as the best part of their lives. All we can conclude from this is that people are different. For me, this world is enough; I'm an atheist and happy to be one. Other people, most likely the majority, are equally happy to be believers. It may be that they need a God to console and reassure themselves, to escape from absurdity or despair (such is the meaning of Kant's 'postulates of practical reason'), or simply to give their lives some sort of coherence; it may be that religion is what they see as the highest part of their lives, either affectively or spiritually – their sensitivity, their education, their history, their thought, their joy, their love . . . All these reasons are worthy of respect. 'Our need for consolation is impossible to satisfy', as Swedish novelist Stig Dagerman once put it. So is our need for love and protection; we all have to deal with these needs as best we can. Mercy upon us.

Mourning and Rituals

What is religion's greatest strength? Contrary to what is often said, it is not the fact that it reassures people on the subject of their own mortality. The perspective of hell is less disturbing than that of nothingness. Such, indeed, was the main thrust of Epicurus's attack on the religions of his day: they give death a reality it doesn't have, thus absurdly locking the living into a purely imaginary danger (hell), which ends up spoiling all life's pleasures for them. Against this, Epicurus taught that 'death is nothing'. It is nothing to the living, since as long as they are alive it does not exist; and nothing to the dead, since *they* no longer exist. To fear death is thus to fear nothing. This doesn't eliminate anxiety (whose very definition, in modern psychiatry, is the fear of a nonexistent object), but it does put it in its place and help us overcome it. What frightens us is our own imagination. What reassures us is our own reason. By definition, there can be nothing to fear in nothingness. To the contrary, what could be more terrifying than the prospect of eternal damnation? True, many of our contemporaries have ceased believing in hell. They see it basically as a metaphor – only heaven, apparently, is to be taken literally. Quite a step forward.

Atheists have none of these worries. We accept our mortality as best we can and try to get used to the idea of nothingness. Can this actually be done? We try not to obsess about it. Death will take everything away with it, including the fear it instils in us. Life on earth is more important to us, and quite sufficient.

Far more real, far more painful and unbearable is the death of loved ones. This is where atheists find themselves the most helpless. The person you care about most – your child, parent, spouse, closest friend – has just been torn away from you by death. How not feel bereft? For you, there can be neither consolation nor compensation – only, sometimes, a faint sense of relief at the thought that at least that person is no longer suffering; at least they need no longer endure the horror, the rending, the terrible pain . . . It takes a long time for the pain to attenuate and become tolerable. Gradually, however, the idea of the person one has lost evolves from gaping wound to piercing nostalgia, to moving memory, to gratitude, and almost to happiness . . . At first, you thought: 'How dreadful that (s)he should no longer be here!' But as the years go by, you start thinking, 'How wonderful that (s)he should have lived, that we should have met, and that we grew to know and love each other!' This is the mourning process: it takes time and memory; it takes acceptance and fidelity. At the moment of the death itself, it is obviously impossible – there is nothing but horror and inconsolable suffering. How one would like to believe in God at such times! How one envies, temporarily, those who do believe! Yes, it must be admitted, this is where religions are virtually unbeatable. Is that any reason to believe? For some people, it clearly is. For others, including myself, it would almost be an additional reason to doubt, either because the ploy seems too obvious or else out of pride, rage and despair. Despite the pain we must endure, mourning merely reinforces our atheism. In the face of terrible distress, we consider revolt more appropriate than prayer; horror, truer than consolation. For us, serenity will come later. Mourning is not a race.

There is another aspect to mourning, an aspect that involves not thoughts but acts, or, more accurately, gestures, and a specific, valued way of performing these gestures together. What religion affords us, when we lose a loved one, is not only the possibility of consolation but also a sorely needed ritual – a ceremony, with or without pomp, a sort of ultimate courtesy, which helps us confront and integrate death (both psychologically and socially), perhaps accept it as well, since we shall eventually have to do so, or at least acknowledge it. Wakes, funeral orations, chants, prayers, symbols, postures, rites, sacraments . . . All these things help us grow accustomed to the horror, humanize it, civilize it – and this is no doubt necessary. A human being can't be buried like an animal or burned like a log. Ritual acknowledges, emphasizes and confirms the difference; that is what makes it almost indispensable. Funerals fulfil with respect to death the same purpose as marriage (for those who deem it necessary) with respect to love and sexuality.

Nothing prevents atheists from seeking an equivalent – and, indeed, they often do so. This has been the case for marriage for quite some time now, with varying degrees of success: civil weddings, when they are not slapdash affairs, offer an acceptable substitute for religious weddings. The idea is to render official the most private, secret, savage part of ourselves – and find some way of including family, friends, society itself. The town hall is sometimes adequate. A party can complete the picture. But where death is concerned? Technically, of course, it is possible for funerals to be a purely civil affair; burials and cremations per se do not require religion. A moment of silence and contemplation could suffice. Silence and tears could suffice. Yet it must be admitted that they rarely do; a nonreligious funeral almost always seems flat, artificial and impoverished – like a poor copy of the original. Perhaps it is a matter of time – two thousand years of emotion and imagery can't be replaced at the drop of a hat – but there is probably more to it than that. The power of religion at such times is neither more nor less than our own powerlessness in the face of the void. *This* is what makes it essential to so many people. If necessary, they could do without hope for themselves. Faced with the unbearable loss of a loved one, however, they cannot do without consolation and ritual. Churches are there for them. They are not about to become obsolete.

'I believe in God,' a reader once told me, 'because life would be too sad without him.' This is not an argument, of course ('It is possible,' as philosopher Joseph-Ernest Renan said, 'that the truth is sad'), but it should be taken into account. There is no reason to take faith away from those who need it – or even those who simply live better because they have it. Some believers are admirable (and the fact that there are more saintly people among believers than among atheists, while it proves nothing as to the existence of God, should make us refrain from scorning religion); most are worthy of respect. Their faith in no way offends me. Why should I combat it? My intention is not to convert people to atheism. It is merely to explain my position and the arguments in its favour, motivated more by the love of philosophy than by the hatred of religion. There are free spirits on both sides, and it is to them that my words are addressed. The others, whether believers or atheists, can be left to their certainties.

Can we do without religion? From an individual point of view, we've seen that the answer to this question is at once simple and subtle: many people, including myself, live perfectly well without it on an everyday basis, and as best they can when confronted with death. This does not imply that everyone should do the same. Atheism is neither a duty nor a requirement. The same is true of religion. It remains for us to accept our differences. When the question is considered in this light, tolerance is the only satisfying answer.

No Society Can Do Without Communion . . .

The word *we* can also refer to a collectivity, a society or even humanity as a whole. Our question then takes on a very different meaning, not so much individual as sociological. It amounts to asking whether or not a society can do without religion.

In this case, it is less a matter of *whom* than *what* we are talking about – in other words, it depends on what we mean by *religion*. Taking the word in its restricted, Western sense – as the belief in a personified creator God – the question has been historically resolved: yes, societies can and do dispense with religion. Confucianism, Taoism and Buddhism have been proving as much for centuries; great societies and admirable civilizations, some of the most ancient and refined among those alive today, recognize no God of this kind.

On the other hand, if the word *religion* is taken in its broader, ethnological sense, the question remains open. As far back as we can go in history, no society has ever been completely without it. The twentieth century is no exception. Nazism laid claim to God (*'Gott mit uns'*). As for the examples of the Soviet Union, Albania or Communist China, they are inconclusive, to say the least – and, indeed, not completely without their messianic or idolatrous traits (the term 'religion of History' has often been used in connection with them, and justifiably so). Moreover, since they did not last long enough to make up a true civilization, or even – fortunately! – to entirely destroy the civilizations that gave rise to them, we can only acknowledge that there has never been a great civilization without sacred myths and rituals, beliefs in certain invisible or supernatural forces – in a word, without religion in the larger, ethnological sense of the word.

Should this lead us to assume that such will always be the case? That would be jumping to conclusions. Spirituality is like the stock exchange: its future can't be predicted on the basis of its past. Still, I'm fairly certain that a few centuries down the line, say, in the year 3000, religions will still exist, and so will atheists. In what proportions? No one can say – and, indeed, that is not the most important question. Our wish is to understand, not to predict.

Etymology can help us, despite (or perhaps thanks to) its uncertainty in the present case.

What is the origin of the word *religion*, a word common to most Western languages? Throughout the history of ideas, two answers have vied with one another, and, as far as I know, modern linguistics has never managed to decide between them. Neither is certain; both are enlightening; more enlightening still, perhaps, is the wavering between the two.

The answer most frequently cited seems to me the most dubious one. Many authors, beginning with Lactantius or Tertullian, claim that the Latin *religio* (whence, of course, *religion*) comes from the verb *religare*, which means 'to bind' or 'bind back'. This hypothesis, often presented as simple fact, leads to a specific conception of religious reality – religion, it is claimed, is *what binds people together*. This hardly constitutes proof that the only conceivable social bond is the belief in God. History, as we have seen, has proved the opposite. Still, it remains true that no society can dispense with bonds among its members. If, therefore, as this etymology suggests, all bonds are assumed to be religious, then no society can dispense with religion. QED. However, this is less a demonstration than it is a tautology (if the two words *religion* and *bond* are synonymous) or a sophism (if they are not). Even clearly established etymologies prove nothing (why would language be 'right'?) – and, as I said, this one happens to be uncertain. Not only that, but to claim that all bonds are religious is to empty the word *religion* of any and all specific working meaning. Self-interest also binds members of a society together, particularly in a market economy; this hardly implies that we should sacralize it, or turn the marketplace into a religion.

True, in monotheistic cultures, people are bound together (horizontally, so to speak) by the fact that all of them feel bound to God (vertically). It is like the warp and woof of the religious material. The community of believers – whether the Chosen People, the Church or the *Umma* – is as powerful as this double bond is solid. What is its real content, however, from the point of view of human sciences? It can only be a human phenomenon – at once psychological, historical and social. What binds believers together, as seen by an outside observer, is not God, whose existence is open to doubt; rather, it is their communion within the same faith. Such, according to Durkheim and most sociologists, is indeed the true content or primary function of religion – it favours social cohesion by reinforcing communion of thought and adhesion to the rules of the group. Fear of retribution or rumour does not suffice, nor does general interest. Indeed, neither of these factors is dependable; witnesses are not always available, and people's interests diverge as often as they coincide. Something else is needed – a cohesion that is more profound, more essential and more durable, thanks to the fact that it is more interior (or interiorized). This is what I mean by communion. How could any society do without it? It would mean renouncing the idea of connection, the idea of community, and thus the idea of society *itself* – for it is communion that creates the community, far more than the other way round. It is not an already-existing community that generates communion; rather, it is a communion that turns a human group into a community, instead of a series of juxtaposed and competing individualities. A people is more than a horde. A society is more, and better, than a multitude.

It remains for us to explore what is meant by communion. Here is how I define it: to commune is to share without dividing. This may sound paradoxical. Where material goods are concerned, it is indeed impossible. People cannot commune in a cake, for instance, because the only way to share it is to divide it. The more people there are, the smaller each person's portion will be, and if one person has more, the others will have less. In a family or a group of friends, on the other hand, people can commune in the pleasure they take in eating a delicious cake together: all share the same delectation, but without having to divide it up! If five or six people are sharing the cake, they can enjoy it as much as if each of them were eating it alone – more, in fact, for in a group of friends the enjoyment of each is enhanced by the enjoyment of all! True, their stomachs will receive smaller portions, but their mental enjoyment will be increased, paradoxically enough, by the very fact of sharing. This is why we talk about communion of minds – because only the mind knows how to share without dividing.

The same is true, *mutatis mutandis*, of societies and states. It is impossible, at least from an accountant's point of view, to commune in a national budget. If you allocate more funds to agriculture, there will be less for education and industry; if you give more to unemployment, there will be less for salaries and retirement pensions; and so forth. On the other hand, in a democratic society that is cohesive, as it should be, it is possible to commune in the love of one's country, in freedom, in solidarity – that is, in a number of shared values that give *meaning* to the budget and make it something different from power struggles, lobbying or arithmetic. The fact that these values are shared by a great number of individuals, as is obviously desirable, by no means diminishes their importance for each. Just the opposite! Each of us is all the more attached to them because we know that other people, who belong to the same community as we do, are also attached to them. The sense of belonging and cohesion go hand in hand. This is what is called a culture or a civilization – a historically and socially determined communion of minds, on the scale of one or several peoples. Without it, there would be no peoples, only individuals. There would be no societies, only crowds and power struggles.

A people is a community. This implies that the individuals who comprise it *commune* in something. Though their communion is always uneven and relative, and always conflictual, too (civilization is not a 'long quiet river'), it is none the less necessary – or, rather, it is *all the more* necessary. Without it, no society can develop, or even subsist. Law is not enough. Repression is not enough. We cannot put a police officer behind every individual. And even if we could, whom would we put behind the police officers? Democracy and public order are all well and good, but neither can replace communion; both are rooted in it.

There is no such thing as a society without bonds, without communion. This by no means implies that all forms of communion, and thus all forms of society, require belief in a personified creator God – or even belief in transcendent, supernatural forces. Do they require belief in something sacred? It all depends on how the word is defined.

If the word *sacred* implies a relationship to the supernatural or the divine, we simply find ourselves in the preceding situation, and modern society can get along fine without it. Elections are preferable to anointments; progress is preferable to sacrament and sacrifice (offering up animals or human beings in holocaust, as many ancient civilizations did, to propitiate invisible powers). Agamemnon, to persuade the gods to give him strong winds, ordered that his daughter Iphigenia's throat be cut. To our way of thinking, this is neither more nor less than crime explained away by superstition. History (the Enlightenment in particular) has rid us of these customs, and it is so much the better. To our eyes, gris-gris have more to do with superstition than with spirituality, and holocausts are more evocative of horror than religion.

If, on the other hand, the word *sacred* implies the existence of a value that is or seems absolute, that imposes itself unconditionally and can be violated only on pain of sacrilege or dishonour (as we refer to the 'sacred' nature of the human individual, or the 'sacred' duty to defend one's country, justice and so forth), then it is likely that no society can do without it for long. Taken in this sense, the sacred is that which would justify, if necessary, the sacrifice of our lives. This is no longer the sacred of sacrificial priests; rather, it is that of heroes (who give up their lives) or that of fine human beings (who under certain circumstances would be prepared to do so). It is that specific dimension of the human species – call it lofty, absolute or noble, as you wish – which, thanks to civilization, makes us different from and greater than animal species. Obviously, we can only be glad of this. But it requires neither a particular metaphysics nor, properly speaking, a religious faith! Humanity, freedom and justice are not supernatural entities. Thus, atheists can respect them – and even give up their lives for them – just as well as believers can. An ideal is not a god. An ethics does not make a religion.

Let us conclude on this point. No society can do

without communion, but (unless religion is defined as communion, which would make one of the two words superfluous) all communion is not religious; it is possible to commune in something other than the divine and the sacred. Conversely (and this, to me, is what matters most), whereas societies can definitely do without god(s) and perhaps without religions, no society can dispense for any length of time with communion.

... or Without Fidelity

The second suggested etymology of *religion* seems to me the more probable one: many linguists believe, as did Cicero, that the word derives not from *religare* but from *relegare*, which means 'to contemplate' or 'to reread'. In this sense, religion is not, or at least not primarily, what binds, but rather what is contemplated or reread (or reread in contemplation) – namely, myths, founding texts, teachings (Torah in Hebrew), a body of knowledge (Veda in Sanskrit), one or several books (*biblia* in Greek), a reading or recitation (Koran in Arabic), a law (*dharma* in Sanskrit), a set of principles, rules or commandments (the Decalogue in the Old Testament) – in a word, a revelation or tradition that is at once ancient and still relevant, accepted, respected, interiorized, both individually and communally. This is where the two possible etymologies can converge: rereading the same texts, even individually, binds people together. In this sense, religion is a factor of integration (for the group) and structure (for the individual and the community). According to this etymology, religion owes less to sociology than it does to philology. It is a love of the Word, the Law or the Book – a love of *Logos*.

The bond still exists, but it is diachronic rather than synchronic – in other words, it connects the present to the past, the living to the dead, piety to tradition or revelation. All religions are *archaic* in the threefold, nonpejorative etymological sense of the word: they are ancient (*arkhaios*) beginnings (*arkhē*) that command (*arkhein*). 'Where will our rebirth come from?' asked Simone Weil. And she replied: 'Only from the past, provided we love it.' It would be a mistake to see this as a reactionary political statement. The issue here is not politics but spirituality and civilization. This is just the opposite of barbarism, which advocates making a clean slate of the past. It is just the opposite of the lack of culture, which knows only the present. 'Mind,' as Saint Augustine put it, 'is memory.' This is as true of peoples as it is of individuals.

If we adopt this etymology, religion has less to do with communion (which binds) than it does with fidelity (which contemplates and rereads); more accurately, it involves the former only thanks to the latter. It is only by contemplating, repeating and rereading the same words, myths or texts (depending on whether the culture is an oral or a written one) that people end up communing in the same beliefs and ideals. *Relegare* is what produces or renders possible *religare*; we are bound together because we reread.

The bond can be created (*within* each generation) only if it has first been transmitted (*from* the preceding generation). In this sense, civilization always precedes itself. It is only possible to meditate together (to commune) if something has first been taught, repeated or reread. There is no such thing as society without education, civilization without transmission, communion without fidelity.

I have chosen the word *fidelity* intentionally – because it is a *doublet*, as the linguists say, of the word *faith*: the two words have the same etymological origin, namely the Latin *fides* – but of course, in modern usage, two different meanings. I find their common origin and divergent development enlightening. They tell me something about our history, and about my own life. Fidelity is what remains when faith has been lost. This accurately describes my own position. I ceased believing in God long ago. Our society, in Europe at least, believes in him less and less. This is no reason, to use the jaded proverb, to throw the baby out with the bathwater. Renouncing a God who has met his social demise (as a Nietzschean sociologist might put it) does not compel us to renounce the moral, cultural and spiritual values that have been formulated in his name. We all know that, historically speaking, these values grew out of the great religions (and specifically, in our own civilizations, the three great monotheisms). There is no denying that they were transmitted by these religions for centuries (and specifically, in our countries, by the Catholic and Protestant churches). This does not prove, however, that these values need God in order to subsist. On the contrary, everything tends to prove that *we* need *them* – an ethics, a sense of communion and fidelity – in order to subsist in a way we find humanly acceptable.

Faith is a belief; fidelity, in the sense I give the word, is more like an attachment, a commitment, a gratitude. Faith involves one or several gods; fidelity involves values, a history, a community. The former calls on imagination or grace; the latter on memory and will.

Of course, faith and fidelity can go hand in hand – this is what I call piety, which is the legitimate goal of believers. They can also come separately, however. This is what distinguishes impiety (the absence of faith) from nihilism (the absence of fidelity). It would be a mistake to confuse the two! When faith is lost, fidelity remains. When both are lost, only the void remains – or calamity.

Frankly, do you need to believe in God to be convinced that sincerity is preferable to dishonesty, courage to cowardice, generosity to egoism, gentleness and compassion to violence and cruelty, justice to injustice, love to hate? Of course not! Those who believe in God recognize these values in God – or perhaps God in them. Such is the traditional set-up: people's faith and their fidelity go hand in hand, and I wouldn't dream of holding it against them. But why shouldn't those of us who are without faith be able to recognize the human grandeur of these values – their urgent importance, their vital necessity, their extreme fragility – and respect them because of all these qualities?

Let us perform a mental experiment. I am now addressing

those believers who, like myself, have children past adolescence (my own are young adults). Imagine what would happen if you lost your faith. Anything is possible . . . In all likelihood, you would want to talk the matter over with your loved ones, at the dinner table for instance, and with your children in particular. What would you tell them? If faith and fidelity were indissociable, as some people claim they are, the speech you would need to make would go something like this. 'Children, I've undergone an astonishing metamorphosis: I don't believe in God any more! So I wanted to let you know, with the utmost solemnity, that all the values I've tried so hard to inculcate into you throughout your childhood and adolescence should henceforth be considered as sheer rubbish!'

Though conceivable in the abstract, this position is highly unlikely. The speech you would make if faced with this sort of situation would probably be a very different one – indeed, quite the opposite. It might go something like this: 'Children, I have something important to tell you: I've lost my faith; I no longer believe in God! Of course, this doesn't in the least affect the values I've always tried to inculcate into you; I'm counting on you to go on respecting them!' Where is the believer who wouldn't deem the second speech more acceptable than the first – from a moral but also from a religious point of view? If you cease believing in God, are you obliged to turn into a coward, a hypocrite, a beast? Of course not! Faith, unfortunately, does not always guarantee fidelity, but the absence of faith by no means precludes it. Indeed, theologically speaking, faith is a God-given grace. Fidelity is more likely a responsibility (though a liberating one), for which it suffices to be human. You can eliminate the former without demeaning yourself; not the latter. Whether or not you have a religion, humanly speaking, ethics continue to prevail.

What sort of ethics? We do not have a great deal of choice in the matter. Even if ethics are human and relative, as I believe them to be, they do not result from decisions or creations. We all find them in ourselves to the extent that we have received them (whether from God, nature or education matters little in the final analysis), and we can criticize one of their facets only by invoking another. For instance, we can invoke individual freedom to condemn the morals governing sexual behaviour, or invoke justice to restrain freedom. All ethics come down to us from the past: for society, they are rooted in history, and for individuals, in childhood. In Freudian terminology, the superego represents the past of the society, just as the id represents the past of the species. This by no means prevents us from criticizing our parents' ethics (indeed, freedom to criticize is one of the values that have been handed down to us), nor does it prevent us from making changes and innovations; but we know quite well that we can do so effectively only by relying on what we have received. As the scriptures put it, our goal should be not so much to destroy our inheritance as to fulfil it.

Nihilism and Barbarism

Nihilism plays into the hands of the barbarians. There are two types of barbarism, however, which it is important not to conflate: the first, irreligious, is merely a generalized or triumphant nihilism; the second, fanaticized, attempts to impose its faith on others through the use of force. Nihilism leads to the former and leaves the field open to the latter.

Nihilistic barbarism has no programme, no ideal, no ideology. It has no need of these things. Its advocates believe in nothing; they know only violence and egotism, contempt and hatred. They are prisoners of their own instincts, their own stupidity and lack of culture, and slaves to what they think of as their freedom. They are barbaric because they lack faith and/or fidelity; they are the mercenaries of the void.

Fanatic barbarism is of a different ilk. Far from lacking faith, its advocates are filled with certainty, enthusiasm and dogmatism; they mistake their faith for knowledge and are prepared to kill or die in its name. They have no doubts or hesitations. They know everything there is to know about Truth and Goodness. Of what use is science to them? Of what use democracy? Everything worth knowing is in the Book. One need only believe and obey. Between Darwin and Genesis, human rights and the Sharia, the rights of peoples and the Torah, they have taken sides once and for all.

They are on God's side. How can they be wrong? Why should they believe in or obey anything else? Fundamentalism. Obscurantism. Terrorism. They see themselves as angels, but behave like beasts or tyrants. They take themselves for the Knights of the Apocalypse. They are the janissaries of the absolute, which they reduce to the narrow dimensions of their own good conscience and perceive as their private property. They are prisoners of their faith, slaves of God or of what (with no proof whatsoever) they claim to be his Word or Law. Spinoza summed them up admirably when he said, 'They fight for their servitude as if it were their salvation.' They see themselves as submitted to God. More power to them, provided they don't infringe upon our freedom by attempting to submit *us* as well!

What is the worst thing that could be imagined? A war between the two fanaticisms. And/or finding ourselves helpless to oppose the various fanaticisms, on the one hand, and nihilism, on the other. In that case, barbarism would take the day; it would matter little whether it came from North or South, East or West, whether it spoke in the name of God or the Void. It is doubtful that our planet would survive.

The opposite of barbarism is civilization. What is needed is not, as Nietzsche recommended, the 'overthrow of all values' – or even, for the most part, the invention of new ones. True values are well known; the Law is well known. Some twenty-six centuries ago, in all the great civilizations that existed at the time, humanity 'selected' (as Darwinians would say) the great values that enable us to live together. Karl Jaspers called this period the axial age (from the Greek *axios*, value), and it is an age to which we all remain indebted. Who would want to go back to the days before Heraclitus or Confucius, Buddha or Lao-tzu, Zoroaster or Isaiah? Should we be content with repeating what they said? Of course not. We should, however, do everything in our power to understand it, bring it up to date, and pass it on! If we do not, there can be no hope of progress.

As several philosophers have demonstrated (Alain in France, Hannah Arendt in the United States), only by transmitting the past to our children can we enable them to invent their future; only by being culturally conservative can we be politically progressive. This is particularly true of ethics, and it applies to values both ancient (those conceived by the great religions and the wise men of old – namely, justice, compassion and love . . .) and modern (those of the Enlightenment – namely, democracy, the separation of church and state, human rights . . .). Let us not make a clean slate of the past! With few exceptions, there is no need to invent new values. What we need to invent, or rather reinvent, is a new fidelity to the values that have been handed down to us, which it is our responsibility to pass on. In effect, we have contracted a debt to the past that can be repaid only to the future. The only way to be truly faithful to the values we have inherited is to pass them on to our children. These two concepts – *transmission* and *fidelity* – are indissociable; the former carries towards the future what the latter has received from the past. They are the two poles of all living traditions – and thus of all civilizations as well. Only by moving ahead can the river of humanity avoid betraying its source.

What Remains of the Christian West When It Ceases to Be Christian?

To recapitulate: a society can do without religion in the restricted, Western sense of the word (the belief in a personal creator God). It might be able to do without the sacred or the supernatural (religion in the broader sense of the word). It cannot, however, do without communion or fidelity.

This is true of all civilizations. The question would be equally valid if we lived in China, India or Iran, only we would discuss it in different terms. We happen to live in the Western world. It is important to acknowledge this important geographical and historical fact. That our civilization is profoundly rooted in the Greco-Roman and Judeo-Christian traditions is something with which I am perfectly comfortable. That it has become nonreligious pleases me even more. It is important, however, that its nonreligiousness be more than just an empty shell or an elegant form of amnesia or denial – something like a refined nihilism, which would amount to a form of decadence. Concretely, this means that the crucial question in our part of the world is the following one: what remains of the Christian West when it ceases to be Christian?

There are only two possible answers to this question: nothing or something.

If we believe that nothing remains, we might as well throw in the towel at once. We would have nothing left to oppose to either fanaticism from without or to nihilism from within – and, contrary to what many people seem to think, nihilism is the primary danger. We would belong to a dead civilization, or at least a dying one. We could go on selling cars and computers, films and video games, but these activities would be meaningless and would not last long – because humanity would no longer be able to recognize itself in them or consider them a sufficient reason to go on living and struggling; hence, it would be unable to resist disaster (whether ideological, ecological or economic). Wealth has never sufficed to make a civilization; poverty, even less so. Civilizations require culture, imagination, enthusiasm and creativity, and none of these things comes without courage, work and effort. 'The main danger that threatens Europe,' as Edmund Husserl put it, 'is fatigue.' Goodnight, little ones; the Western world has decided to replace faith with somnolence.

We can also believe, however, that something does remain of the Christian West when it ceases to be Christian. And given that what remains is no longer a common faith (since it has objectively ceased to be common – 50 per cent of the French population today is either atheist, agnostic or nonreligious, some 8 per cent are Muslim, and so forth), it can only be a common fidelity, that is, a shared attachment to the values we have inherited, which, for each of us, presupposes or entails the desire to pass them on.

To believe or not to believe in God – the question is a crucial one for individuals. (I shall address it in my second chapter.) For peoples, however, it is not the main thing. The destiny of our civilization cannot depend on a question that is objectively insoluble! There are more important, more urgent issues to be dealt with. Indeed, even for individuals, the question of faith should not obfuscate the more decisive question of fidelity. Do I really wish to subject my conscience to a belief (or unbelief) that cannot be verified? Do I really wish to derive my morals from my metaphysics and measure my duties against my faith? That would mean giving up a certainty for an uncertainty, an actually existing humanity for an only possibly existing God. This is why I sometimes like to describe myself as a *faithful atheist*. I am an atheist, since I believe neither in God nor in any supernatural power, and yet I am faithful, since I acknowledge my place within a specific history, tradition and community, namely the Greco-Judeo-Christian values of the Western world.

My adolescence prepared me for this. I was a Christian back then, as I have said, but I did not spend all my time studying the catechism. In that phase of my existence, the person who taught me the most about ethics – more than any priest and for a long time more than any philosopher – was the singer Georges Brassens. Everyone knew he did not believe in God, yet his ethics, though admittedly not in conformity with those of the Vatican, bore the imprint of the Gospels and remained essentially faithful to them, conveying what philosopher Jean-Marie Guyau has described as an ethics 'with neither obligation nor punishment'. Perhaps the songs of Joan Baez, Woody Guthrie or the Beatles played a similar role in the English-speaking world.

Another important mentor in my life has been Montaigne, though I did not discover him until much later. Whether or not he believed in God is a matter of debate among specialists. He mentioned Socrates more often than Abraham, and Lucretius more often than Jesus. More than anything, he taught freedom. This did not prevent him, when discussing moral issues, from quoting Genesis ('the first law God ever gave man') or mentioning the Ten Commandments, 'which Moses drew up for the people of Judea come out of Egypt'. His mother, apparently, was Jewish. Perhaps this helped him see that there is no contradiction between fidelity and spiritual freedom.

The same was true of Spinoza. He was no more a Christian than I am; indeed, he may well have been as much of an atheist as I am (he did not, at least, believe in any transcendent God) – and yet he thought of Jesus as a great master. Was he God? Definitely not. Was he the Son of God? No, not that, either. For Spinoza, Jesus was merely a human being, but an exceptional one – 'the greatest of all philosophers', he once called him – the one who best expressed the essence of morality. And what might that be? What Spinoza calls 'the spirit of Christ', namely, that for free spirits the only law is 'justice and charity', the only wisdom is love, and the only virtue is to 'do good and live in joy'. Why should my atheism prevent me from seeing the greatness of this message?

Christian Atheist or Integrated Goy?

To illustrate what I mean by fidelity, I would like to share a few stories with you – or, rather, two memories, one joke and one story.

Let me begin with the most recent memory. It dates back some fifteen years, to an interdisciplinary colloquium held in Salzburg, Austria, on the evolution of our societies. One of the debates in which I took part was run by Jean Boissonnat, then editor-in-chief of a major French economic journal. Without concealing my atheism, I approached the day's topic from the perspective of what I now call fidelity, drawing my references not only from Montaigne, Rousseau, Kant and Wittgenstein but also, more surprisingly, from the Old and New Testaments, which I commented on in my own way, sometimes quoting from Thomas Aquinas, Pascal or Kierkegaard. Surprised by this orientation, admittedly a quirky one on the French intellectual scene, Boissonnat finally exclaimed, 'When you come right down to it, Mr Comte-Sponville, you're a Christian atheist!' I found the expression too self-contradictory to be acceptable. 'Christians believe in God, and I do not,' I replied, 'so I'm not a Christian. What I am – or at least what I try to be – is a faithful atheist.' Unless I am mistaken, that was the first time the expression crossed my lips.

Back in Paris a few days later, I told a friend about this exchange, quoting Boissonnat's term for me and describing my own surprise and response to it. Here was my friend's reaction: 'It doesn't matter whether you call yourself a Christian atheist or a faithful atheist; when you come right down to it, Boissonnat is right! Look at our Jewish friends – many of them describe themselves as "atheistic Jews". What do they mean by that? Not that they have Judaism in their genes – that would be scientifically debatable and most of them could not care less about their genes. No, what they mean is that they don't believe in God – thus, they are atheistic – but still consider themselves to be Jewish. Why? Not because of genes, which are irrelevant in this case; not because of faith, which they don't have; and not *only* (sorry, Sartre!) because of anti-Semitism. No, if they feel Jewish, it's because they recognize and value their appurtenance to a specific history, tradition and community. Well, just as they claim to be "atheistic Jews", you can claim to be an "atheistic Christian" or a "Christian atheist"!'

I did not follow this friend's advice, for fear that it might lead to confusion or misunderstanding. In its essence, however, and despite obvious differences (there is no equivalent in Christian history of the Diaspora, the Shoah or Israel), his reasoning was accurate. I do feel attached to the

Christian (or Judeo-Christian) tradition, in much the same way as my atheistic Jewish friends are attached to their own communities. Indeed, some of them have helped me to understand just this – which leads me to my second story.

It took place several years before the first. I was teaching philosophy in a provincial high school. I happened to be back in Paris one day and, strolling down the Boulevard Saint-Michel, I ran into an old college mate of mine with whom I'd been out of touch for a number of years. We decided to have a cup of coffee together on the Place de la Sorbonne. Standing at the bar, we gave each other a run-down of what we'd been doing since we'd last met – I taught first here, then there, got married, had children, published such-and-such a book . . .

Then my friend added, 'There's something else. I attend synagogue now.'

'Were you Jewish?'

'I still am!'

'You never mentioned it! How would I have known?'

'Given my name . . .'

'You know, apart from Levy or Cohen, names don't mean much to people who are neither Jewish nor anti-Semitic.'

Back in the days when we were students together, my friend had been one of those Jews who were so integrated that it didn't seem to be an issue at all, either religiously (most of them were atheists), ethnically (all of them were anti-racists) or culturally (almost all of them were universalists). They felt Jewish, as a number of them had explained to me, only to the extent that other people were anti-Semitic – and in our milieu at the time, either anti-Semites were few and far between or else they kept a very low profile! As far as I can recall, this friend was no exception to the rule. He'd never mentioned religion or Judaism in the course of our student years. People thought of him as an atheist or an agnostic – and, like almost all of us, he probably was. Having gradually moved away from the Maoism of his youth, he had become interested in Kant and phenomenology. I had not known that he was Jewish, and it would have seemed irrelevant to me at the time. Why would nonbelievers discuss the faith they didn't have? Now here he was, barely ten years later, attending synagogue! Surprised by this development, I questioned him about what I saw as its most salient feature.

'You mean you believe in God now?'

My friend smiled at me disarmingly.

'For Jews,' he replied, 'believing or not believing in God isn't the main issue.'

I was nonplussed. For someone raised in the Catholic tradition like me, believing or not believing in God was practically the *only* issue! My friend went on to explain why this was not the case for him. Why attach so much importance, he asked me, to a question we can never resolve – and over which we have no control? Isn't it preferable to deal with things we know about and that depend on us? Still smiling, he quoted the well-known Jewish quip: 'God doesn't exist, but we're his Chosen People.' In short, my friend explained to me that for Jews, or for him at least, the attachment to a specific history, tradition, Law, Book – and thus to a specific community – was far more important than the contingent (or at least secondary) matter of believing or not believing in God. Also, he was a father now, and he cared about passing his recently rediscovered inheritance on to his children. 'Judaism,' he insisted, 'is the only religion in which the first duty of parents is to teach their children to read – so that they can read the Torah.'

That friend was the first in a long series. In France, a whole generation of Jews – including those who considered themselves atheists, as most of my friends did – seemed to be re-evaluating their relationship to Judaism, and this gave me food for thought. I came to see that what they thought of as their tradition was also, to a great extent, *our* tradition. If they were justified in returning to it, exploring it and laying claim to it, even without believing in God, might there not be some degree of stupidity in the contempt we liked to show for it? Might it not be worth wondering how it happened that the Jewish people – though for so many centuries they had had no state, no land, no structure other than memory and fidelity – had shown such enormous creativity and freedom of spirit and made such an extraordinary contribution to scientific and human progress?

As I walked home after that conversation, I suddenly felt as if I had stumbled into uncharted territory.

The term *Judeo-Christian* was pejorative in those days, especially when used as an adjective. Judeo-Christian morality, for instance, was invariably rejected as repressive, castrating and guilt-inducing. Nietzsche and hedonism were the masters of the day. True, they had felt – at first – like a gust of fresh, liberating air. As time went by, however, I began to see this attitude as both unfair and dangerous. 'Is it the word *Judeo* that bothers us,' I wondered, 'or the word *Christian*?' The answer depended on time and place. I personally had to admit, however, that neither of these words bothered me. On the contrary, to the atheist I had become, they represented a double debt of honour or spirit. And so, every now and then – as a form of homage to my Jewish friends, and also out of revulsion for anti-Semites – I began, when asked about my religion, to describe myself as an 'integrated goy'. It was only a joke, of course, but it said something true about what it means to be a faithful atheist in a Judeo-Christian land.

Two Rabbis, a Dalai Lama and a Périgordian

My joke is along much the same lines; it's a Jewish joke. I remember telling it once during a lecture, in a city somewhere in eastern France – Strasbourg, I think it was. During the cocktail party after the conference, the organizers introduced me to several of the city's eminent personalities, including the great rabbi.

As we raised our glasses in a toast, he said to me, 'A funny thing happened during your lecture.'

'Oh? What was that?'

'You were discussing fidelity . . . I leaned over to the person sitting next to me and whispered, "That reminds me of a Jewish joke. I'll tell it to you afterwards." And it was the joke you yourself told just a few seconds later!'

So here is a joke authenticated by none other than the great rabbi of Strasbourg. Two rabbis are having dinner together. They are close friends; they can tell each other anything. All night long they discuss the existence of God and eventually come to the conclusion that God does not exist. At last they go off to bed. In the morning, one of the rabbis gets up, looks for his friend all over the house, doesn't find him, goes to look for him outside – and finds him in the garden, absorbed in his ritual morning prayers.

Surprised, he says, 'Hey! What are you doing?'

'You can see for yourself – I'm saying my ritual morning prayers.'

'That's just what surprises me! We talked halfway through the night, we decided that God did not exist, and here you are saying your ritual morning prayers?'

The other rabbi replies, quite simply, 'What does God have to do with it?'

Jewish humour, Jewish wisdom: what makes us smile is

that it seems strange to go on saying your ritual prayers when you no longer believe in God. But our smile might well conceal – or reveal – an important lesson. Every now and then, when people express surprise at my being faithful to the Judeo-Christian tradition in spite of my atheism, or an atheist in spite of this fidelity, I answer, 'What does God have to do with it?' Let those who have ears (or a sense of humour) hear.

I need scarcely add that one need not be (or have been) either Jewish or Christian to endorse this fidelity. There is no such thing as a chosen people or a mandatory civilization. Had I been born in China, India or Africa, my path would have been a different one, yet it would still imply a form of fidelity (albeit a critical or impious fidelity like my own). Only fidelity can hope to bring forth, over and above the diversity of cultures, what is universally human in each of them – and still more in the encounter *among* them, which is true civilization. 'When you don't know where you're going,' says an African proverb, 'it's important to remember where you came from.' Only memory – history, culture – can help us know where we *want* to go. Progressive thinking and fidelity go hand in hand. The universal is not behind us; it's up ahead. It can be reached only by following a path, and all paths are particular.

I have forgotten just where I came across the last story, but I'm fairly certain the person who told it to me had witnessed it directly. One day, after listening to a lecture by the Dalai Lama in a city somewhere in Europe, a young

Frenchman went up to him and said, 'Your Holiness, I want to convert to Buddhism.' In his great wisdom, the Dalai Lama answered simply, 'Why Buddhism? In France, you've got Christianity. There's nothing wrong with Christianity!' No response could have been more irreligious – or more conducive to fidelity. It reminds me of Montaigne's well-known observation in his *Apology for Raymond Sebond*: 'We are Christian by the same title that we are Périgordians or Germans.' One of the philosopher's best commentators, Marcel Conche, deduces from this that since Montaigne was indisputably from the Périgord, he was just as indisputably Christian. This is no doubt true – but not in a way his church would have found satisfactory (his *Essays* were prohibited by the Index in 1676) or in a way that would help us decide whether or not he believed in God. The declaration itself is ambiguous on this point. It merely suggests (whence its importance) that belief in God is not the most important thing – that fidelity, in the sense I give the word, matters more than faith.

What Difference Does Loss of Faith Make?

This by no means implies that being or becoming an atheist changes nothing at all. I know what I am talking about. Having been a believer throughout the most crucial years of my life, childhood and adolescence, I am in a good position to measure the change brought about by not believing. It is neither absolute nor negligible. Kant himself confirmed as much, from his own standpoint as a pious philosopher. In a famous passage of his *Critique of Pure Reason*, he summed up the sphere of philosophy in three questions: what can I know? What should I do? What may I hope for? Let us briefly confront each of these questions with the possible loss of faith.

Where knowledge is concerned, the loss of faith changes nothing. The sciences remain the same and have the same limitations. Our scientists are well aware of this. Their belief or nonbelief in God might affect the way in which they experience their profession (their moods and motivations, the ultimate meaning of their quest in their own eyes), but it affects neither the results of their research nor its theoretical status. Thus, it should not affect their profession per se (or else it would cease to be scientific). It can change their subjective relationship to knowledge, but not knowledge itself or its objective limits.

Where morals are concerned, the loss of faith changes nothing or next to nothing. That you have lost your faith does not mean that you will suddenly decide to betray your friends or indulge in robbery, rape, assassination and torture. 'If God does not exist,' says Dostoyevsky's Ivan Karamazov, 'everything is allowed.' Not at all, for the simple reason that I will not allow myself everything! As Kant demonstrated, either morals are autonomous or they do not exist at all. If a person refrains from murdering his neighbour only out of fear of divine retribution, his behaviour is dictated not by moral values but by caution, fear of the holy policeman, egoism. And if a person does good only with an eye to salvation, she is not doing good (since her behaviour is dictated by self-interest, rather than by duty or by love) and will thus not be saved. This is Kant, the Enlightenment and humanity at their best: a good deed is not good because God commanded me to do it (in which case it would have been good for Abraham to slit his son's throat); on the contrary, it is because an action is good that it is possible to believe God commanded it. Rather than religion being the basis for morals, morals are now the basis for religion. This is the inception of modernity. To have a religion, the *Critique of Practical Reason* points out, is to 'acknowledge all one's duties as sacred commandments'. For those who no longer have faith, commandments vanish (or, rather, lose their sacred quality), and all that remains are duties – that is, the commandments we impose upon ourselves.

Alain puts it beautifully in his *Letters to Sergio Solmi on the Philosophy of Kant*: 'Ethics means knowing that we are spirit and thus have certain obligations, for *noblesse oblige*. Ethics is neither more nor less than a sense of dignity.' Should I rob, rape and murder? It would be unworthy of me – unworthy of what humanity has become, unworthy of the education I have been given, unworthy of what I am and wish to be. I therefore refrain from such behaviour, and this is what is known as ethics. There is no need to believe in God – one need believe only in one's parents and mentors, one's friends (provided they are well chosen) and one's conscience.

I say that the presence or absence of a religious faith changes 'next to nothing', morally speaking, because on certain issues – having less to do with morals than theology – there are, admittedly, a few minor differences. Take the issue of contraception in general, or the condom in particular. Abortion is a moral issue: it is something that believers and unbelievers alike need to confront, and indeed there are proponents of liberalization, though in different proportions, on both sides of the line. Never, on the other hand, have I seen an atheist involved in heart-searching on the issue of the condom. If you are without religion, the question of whether or not it is morally acceptable to use a condom (either as a means of contraception or – especially – to protect yourself and your partner from AIDS) is easy to answer. The condom is not a moral issue, it's a theological problem (and even that is debatable, since the Gospels have precious little to say on the topic). The same goes, frankly, for people's sexual preferences. There is no need for morals to intervene in sexual behaviour between consenting adults. Homosexuality, for instance, may be a theological issue (the destruction of Sodom and Gomorrah in Genesis suggests as much). It is not, at least not any longer, a moral issue – or, rather, it is a moral issue only for those who insist on confusing morals and religion, particularly if they resort to a literal interpretation of the Bible or the Koran to avoid having to think for themselves. They are free to do so, provided they apply such morals only to themselves and continue to respect the laws of modern democracies (sovereignty of the people, individual freedoms). We, in turn, are free not to follow their example, to combat them if we so desire (again, within legal limits), and, finally, to defend our own freedom of conscience and self-examination. Why should my spirit be subjected to a faith I do not share, a religion in which I do not believe, laws that were formulated hundreds or even thousands of years ago by a tribal chief or warrior? Fidelity, yes – on condition that it be critical, constantly reconsidered, brought up to date. Blind submission, no.

But let us move away from these archaic quarrels. On all the crucial moral issues, believing or not believing in God changes nothing of great significance, except in the eyes of fundamentalists. Whether you have a religion or not, nothing can exempt you from having to respect the lives, freedom and dignity of other people. It is not religion that makes love superior to hatred, generosity to egotism and justice to injustice. That religions, historically speaking, may have helped us understand these values by no means implies that they have a monopoly on them – or that they suffice to implement them. Pierre Bayle summed this up powerfully, as long ago as the late seventeenth century: atheists are as liable to be virtuous as believers are liable *not* to be.

Nihilism and Sophistry: The Two Temptations of Postmodernity

Unfortunately, almost no one reads Bayle in our day and age. Far more fashionable among contemporary intellectuals are de Sade and Nietzsche – whence two temptations, both deleterious, that threaten our modernity from within or turn it into postmodernity: on a theoretical level, the temptation of sophistry, and on a practical level, the temptation of nihilism. I would go along with Régis Debray in saying that postmodernity is modernity minus the Enlightenment. It is a modernity that has ceased to believe in reason or progress (whether political, social or human) and thus in itself. If all value systems are equal, nothing has *any* value: science is a myth among others; progress is an illusion; and a democracy respectful of human rights is in no way superior to a society based on slavery and tyranny. In that case, what remains of the Enlightenment, the belief in progress and civilization?

That progress is neither linear nor inevitable goes without saying. This means that it is worth fighting for (since decadence is always possible), not that we should give up.

I call *sophistry* any and all discourses that hinge on values other than truth or claim that truth hinges on something other than itself. This culminates – or, rather, collapses – in a declaration that, though it might have a Dostoyevskian ring to it, is more Nietzschean in content: 'If God does not exist, then there is no such thing as truth.'

I call *nihilism* any and all discourses that recommend the overthrow or destruction of morals, not on the pretext that they are relative, something I readily acknowledge (sciences, too, are relative, which is no reason to reject them!), but on the pretext that, as Nietzsche claims, they are nefarious and hypocritical. This amounts to endorsing Ivan Karamazov's statement 'If God does not exist, everything is allowed.' Its culmination (or caricature) is the famous May 1968 slogan 'It is forbidden to forbid.' Here we have moved from freedom to licence, from revolt to servility, from relativism to nihilism. This can lead only to decadence or barbarism. No value can prevail, no duty can impose itself; all that remains is my own pleasure or fearfulness, self-interest and power relationships.

These two temptations – sophistry and nihilism – were brilliantly described by Nietzsche, particularly in his later works – and Nietzsche dominates the postmodern age because he had a presentiment of the abyss and occasionally (though never losing his inimitable eloquence) dived into it headfirst. One of his *Posthumous Fragments* sums them up in a single phrase: 'Nothing is true; everything is allowed.'

The first of these propositions is logically untenable. If nothing is true, then it is not true that nothing is true; the phrase destroys itself without refuting itself (if nothing is true, no refutation is possible). This is the defeat of reason. You can think nothing at all – or, rather, you can think *any-thing* at all, which amounts to the same thing. Anything goes, but nothing is meaningful (in philosophy as in the sciences, thought can progress only by encountering impossibility, which is the proof of objectivity; even if there is no such thing as absolute truth, we need to be able to reject errors – that is, statements that *cannot* be true). Reality itself becomes ungraspable. 'There are no facts,' wrote

Nietzsche in another posthumous fragment, 'there are only interpretations.' Or again, as early as *Beyond Good and Evil*: 'The fact that a judgement is false is not, in our view, an objection against that judgement.' This makes Nietzsche irrefutable. It is the triumph of sophistry: for many of our contemporaries, truth is merely the final illusion, and it is time we broke free of it. Naturally, morals cannot survive. If nothing is true, no one is either innocent or guilty of anything, and we can formulate no reproach against negationists, liars, mass murderers (since it is not true that they are such), or ourselves. Whence it can be seen that sophistry necessarily paves the road – and a fine, smooth road it is! – to nihilism.

The threat represented by the second proposition is essentially a moral one. If everything is allowed, we can ask nothing of ourselves and expect nothing of others. There is no reason to combat horror, violence or injustice. All we can do is give in to nihilism and servility (the former being merely the high-class version of the latter), and hand the world over to the fanatics and the barbarians. If everything is allowed, then so are terrorism, torture, dictatorship and genocide. 'The fact that an act is immoral,' such thinkers might say, 'is not, in our view, an objection against that act.' How pleasant for mass murderers and cowards! There is no difference between lies, truth and twaddle. Whence it can be seen that nihilism paves the road – and a very boring road it is! – to sophistry.

True, Nietzsche himself usually found ways to avoid

this double temptation, thanks either to his genius or his aestheticism, that is, the wish to turn his life into a work of art (in the grand style). I am well aware of this and not indifferent to it. Still, apart from its narcissism, Nietzsche's attitude is less a way out than a dead end. People who wish to turn their lives into works of art are deluding themselves about art and lying about life. Look at Oscar Wilde. Look at Nietzsche himself. What a rotten, miserable life he had, when you think about it; and how suspicious, not to say pitiful, this makes Zarathustra's braggadocio sound! However, this is a subject unto itself – one I cannot go into here. I wish only to emphasize that fidelity, in the sense I have given the word, incites us to turn away from the double temptation of nihilism and sophistry. If there were no such thing as truth, there would be no such thing as knowledge, and it would be impossible for knowledge to progress. If there were no such thing as values – or if all values were worthless – there could be no such thing as either human rights or social and political progress. All forms of combat would be vain, as would peace itself.

Today, for atheists in particular, it is crucial to build a double rampart against this double temptation, opposing sophistry with rationalism on the one hand and nihilism with humanism on the other. Taken together, these two ramparts make up what has been known since the eighteenth century as the Enlightenment.

It is not true that nothing is true. Obviously, no body of knowledge can express absolute, eternal and infinite truth.

But knowledge is knowledge only by virtue of the (relative, approximate, historical) truth that it imparts or by virtue of the error that it refutes – whence its ability to progress. Scientific history advances 'by writing over and crossing out', as Jean Cavaillès puts it, 'by trial and error', as Karl Popper puts it – *but it does advance*. Indeed, Gaston Bachelard points out that progress is 'the very dynamic of scientific culture. The history of the sciences is the history of the defeats of irrationalism.' Thus – fidelity to reason, to mind, to knowledge. '*Saper' aude*', as Kant said, following Horace and Montaigne – that is, dare to know, dare to use your intelligence, dare to distinguish the possibly true from the certainly false!

It is not true that anything goes – or, rather, it is up to each and all of us to make it untrue. Thus – fidelity to humanity and to our own duty to be human! This is what I call practical humanism, which is not a religion but an ethic. 'There is nothing so beautiful and legitimate,' Montaigne said, 'as to play the man well and properly.' Yes, to properly play the man – or, since humanity is sexed, the woman – is humanism in action and the very opposite of nihilism. We must try to be worthy of what humanity has made of itself – and thus of what civilization has made of us. Our primary duty, the one from which all the others follow, is that of living and behaving *humanly*.

Religion can neither guarantee that we do so nor exempt us from needing to do so.

Cheerful Despair

We are left with Kant's third question: 'What may I hope for?' In the subject at hand, this is the most important question of all. The loss of faith brings about no transformation in knowledge and almost none in morals. But it considerably changes the degree of hope – or hopelessness – in human existence.

If you believe in God, what may you hope for? Everything, or at least everything that really matters: the ultimate triumph of life over death, justice over injustice, peace over war, love over hate and happiness over unhappiness. 'An infinity of happiness in an infinity of life', as Pascal put it. Philosophically, as I shall explain in the next chapter, I would tend to see this as an objection against religion. Subjectively, however, given the fact that religion is bolstered by hope and indifferent to our reasonings, it predicts a bright future for religion.

What can people hope for who have never believed in God or who have ceased believing in him? Nothing – that is, nothing absolute or eternal, nothing beyond the 'darkest reaches of death', as Gide put it – which means that all our hopes for this life, no matter how legitimate (less war, less suffering, less injustice), run up against that ultimate nothingness; it engulfs all, joy and misery alike. That makes one more injustice (the fact that death strikes innocent and guilty alike) and one more misery, or several (one for each period of mourning in a person's lifetime). It condemns us to seeing life as tragic – or, if we seek oblivion, as entertainment. Such is the world of Lucretius, the world of Camus and our own world: nature is blind; our desires insatiable; only death is immortal. This by no means prevents us from struggling for justice, but it does prevent us from believing in it completely or believing that its triumph can be permanent. In a word, Pascal, Kant and Kierkegaard were right: there is no way for a lucid atheist to avoid despair. This was the subject I addressed in my very first philosophical writings, particularly my *Treatise on Despair and Bliss*. Did I do so because I wished to drown in misery? Quite the opposite! I wished to escape from it and to show that happiness is not something to be hoped for but something to be experienced here and now! This by no means eliminates tragedy. But why should it be eliminated? Far better to accept it as joyfully as possible. Tragic wisdom is the wisdom of happiness and finitude, happiness and impermanence, happiness and despair. This is not as paradoxical as it might sound. You can hope only for what you do not have. Thus, to hope for happiness is to lack it. When you have it, on the other hand, what remains to be hoped for? For it to last? That would mean fearing its cessation, and as soon as you do that, you start feeling it dissolve into anxiety. Such is the trap of hope, with or without God – the hope for tomorrow's happiness prevents you from experiencing today's.

'Would I ever be happy, if only I were happy!' sighs

Woody Allen. But how can he *be* happy, if he goes on hoping to *become* so? We all tend to reason this way. Forever 'gaping after things to come', as Montaigne puts it. Forever dissatisfied. Forever filled with hope and fear. Happiness would mean having what we want. But how can we, if desire is lack? If we want only what we do not have, we can never have what we want. We are cut off from happiness by the very hope that impels us to pursue it; cut off from the present (which is all) by the future (which is nothing). Pascal summed it up brilliantly: 'So it is that, instead of living, we hope to live', and that, 'forever preparing for happiness, it is inevitable we should not know it'. I wanted to break away from that 'inevitable' by working out something I called a wisdom of despair. In the Western tradition, such a wisdom would be akin to that of the first Epicurians or the Stoics, and, later, to Spinoza; in the Eastern tradition, it would derive from Buddhism or the Samkhya. ('Only the despairing can be happy,' says one of the Samkhya Sutras, 'for hope is the greatest torture, and despair the greatest joy.') Once again, this is only superficially contradictory. Wise people wish only for what is or for what depends on them. What good would hope do them? As for foolish people, they wish only for what is not (this is what distinguishes hope from love) and for what does not depend on them (this is what distinguishes hope from will). How can they be happy? They never stop hoping. How can they stop fearing?

'There is no hope without fear,' wrote Spinoza, 'and no

fear without hope.' We usually think of serenity as the absence of fear, but it is also the absence of hope; thus, it frees the present moment for action, knowledge and joy! This attitude has nothing to do with passivity, laziness or resignation. To wish only for what depends on us (to *want*) is to give ourselves the means of making it happen. To wish for what does not depend on us (to *hope*) is to condemn ourselves to powerlessness and resentment. The path is clear enough. The wise act; the foolish hope and tremble. The wise live in the present, wishing only for what is (acceptance, love) or what they can bring about (will). Such, indeed, is the spirit of Stoicism and of Spinoza. Such is the spirit of all wisdom, no matter what the doctrine. It is not hope that spurs us to action (how many people hope for justice but do nothing in its favour?); it is will. It is not hope that sets us free; it is truth. It is not hope that helps us live; it is love.

Thus, despair can be a bracing, healthy, joyous attitude. It is the very opposite of nihilism – or else its antidote. What nihilists feel is not despair but disappointment (and one can be disappointed only with respect to a prior hope); they are weary and embittered, filled with rancour and resentment. They cannot forgive life, or the world, or humanity, for not fulfilling the hopes they had conceived for them. But whose fault is it if their hopes were illusory? People who hope for nothing, on the other hand, cannot be disappointed. People who desire only what is or what depends on them, who are content to love and to will, cannot be weary or embittered. The opposite of rancour is gratitude. The opposite of resentment is mercy. The opposite of nihilism is love and courage.

No one can deny that much about the human condition is appalling. But this is no reason to stop loving life – just the opposite! All trips end eventually. Is that any reason to renounce undertaking one and enjoying it? You only live once. Is that any reason to spoil the single life you do have? Nothing can guarantee the triumph of peace and justice, or even any irreversible progress. Is that any reason to stop fighting for these things? Of course not! On the contrary, it is a powerful reason to go on paying the utmost attention to life, peace, justice . . . and our children. Life is all the more precious for being rare and fragile. Justice and peace are all the more necessary, all the more urgent, because nothing can guarantee their ultimate victory. Humanity is all the more moving for being alone, courageous and loving. 'When you have learned not to hope,' Seneca wrote, 'I shall teach you how to want' – and I would add along with Spinoza, to love.

I wrote a few books on the subject. At the time, I sensed (accurately, I think) that this outlook was at odds with Christianity. 'The opposite of despair is belief,' as Kierkegaard put it. I turned the sentence on its head: 'The opposite of belief is despair.' I coined the phrase *cheerful despair* – a takeoff on what Nietzsche had dubbed 'the cheerful science' – and I still enjoy its bitter but invigorating taste.

Love and the Kingdom

I had reached this point in my thinking some fifteen years ago. Basically, I have not changed since, except on a single point: despite its crucial importance, I am no longer certain that the question of hope is what opposes religion to atheism.

Again, I can illustrate what I mean by telling a story. It happened a few years ago. I had given a lecture, somewhere in the provinces, on the idea of a godless spirituality. Among the people who had come up to chat with me after the lecture was a rather elderly man who introduced himself as a Catholic priest (and I saw there was a small golden cross pinned to his lapel). 'I came to thank you,' he said. 'I enjoyed your lecture very much.' Then he added, 'I agreed with everything you said.'

I thanked him in turn, but could not help adding, 'Still, Father, I must admit it surprises me to hear you say you agreed with everything I said. Surely you can't agree when I say I don't believe in God or the immortality of the soul!'

'Oh,' said the elderly priest with a benevolent smile, 'those are such secondary matters!'

He was talking about the existence of God and the immortality of the soul, and he was a Catholic priest. I have no idea what his bishop would have made of such a declaration, which was unorthodox to say the least. I can guess what fundamentalists, whether Christian or Muslim, would make of it – they would say the man was under the deleterious influence of the devil or relativism. Too bad for them.

For my part, I found these words truly evangelical. Jesus himself may have believed in God and resurrection. What Jew did not, back then? But what was important to me, when I read the Gospels, was less what Jesus said about God or a possible life after death (indeed, he said relatively little on the subject) than what he said about humanity and life on earth. Remember the Good Samaritan. He was neither Jewish nor Christian. We have no idea what his faith was or what he thought about death. All we know is that he showed compassion and charity. And Jesus explicitly told us to imitate *him*, not a priest or a Levite. My encounter with the Catholic priest taught me that the value of human beings has nothing to do with whether or not they believe in God or life after death. On those issues, the only truth (as I shall attempt to show) is that we know nothing at all. Thus, in these areas, believers and unbelievers are separated only by what they do not know. This does not eliminate our disagreements, but it does relativize their importance. It would be madness to attach more significance to what we don't know and what separates us than to what we know from our own experience, in the depths of our hearts, and what brings us together, namely, the idea that people's real worth is measured neither by faith nor hope but by the amount of love, compassion and justice of which they are capable!

Remember the Hymn to Charity, in the First Epistle to the Corinthians. In this beautiful text, Saint Paul invoked what would later come to be called the three theological virtues: faith, hope and charity (or love, *agapē*). The greatest of the three, Saint Paul explained, is charity. I can have the gift of languages, the gift of prophecy, the ability to move mountains; if I do not have love, I am nothing. Moreover, he added, in substance, all the rest will end eventually; only 'charity never faileth'. Many of us have read or heard this text dozens of times without wondering what it meant. Fortunately, certain great minds have incited us to think about it. Rereading this passage, Saint Augustine asked himself, *Does Paul mean to say that faith and hope will eventually fail?* And faced with that question, he answered yes on at least two occasions (in Sermon 158 and *Soliloquies* 1.7).

Faith will pass: in the kingdom of heaven, it will no longer be necessary to believe in God, since we shall *be* in God, know him and see him, as Saint Paul told us, face to face. 'It will no longer be faith but sight,' Augustine wrote. But our love will be all the greater: 'If we love now, believing without seeing, how could we not love then, when we shall see and possess?'

Hope will pass: in heaven, by definition, the blessed will have nothing left to hope for. They will possess the very thing they now hope for (namely, that God be 'everything in all'), so 'it will no longer be a hope but reality'.

Love will continue to exist, or rather it will exist all the more: 'Charity, then, will be perfect.'

Thus, in the kingdom of heaven, faith and hope are destined to disappear: 'Why would we need faith, since our souls will see? And why would we need hope, since they will possess?' Hope and faith are temporary virtues, meaningful only for life on earth. 'After this life,' added Saint Augustine, 'when the soul is completely absorbed by God, only love will remain to keep it there.' He went on to explain: 'We can no longer say that the soul has faith, that it believes in these truths, since no deceptive evidence will attempt to distract it from them; nor will it need to hope, since it will possess everything that is good in complete security.' From this, it logically follows that, as Saint Augustine puts it very simply, 'The three virtues of faith, hope and charity are all necessary in this life; but after this life charity alone will suffice.'

Therefore, Saint Paul is right. In the kingdom of heaven, faith and hope will have disappeared; only charity, or love, will remain!

From my own standpoint as a faithful atheist, I would simply add that this is already true. Why dream about paradise? The kingdom is here and now. It is up to us to inhabit a material and spiritual space (the world, our bodies: the present) in which we have nothing to believe but everything to learn, nothing to hope for but everything to do (for those things we can change) or to love (for those we cannot).

Do not get me wrong. I am not insinuating that Saint Augustine was an atheist like me – he most definitely was not! All I wish to suggest is that, for those believers who think that we are already, at least partly, in the kingdom, this kingdom is by definition something we share; thus only hope and faith, not love or knowledge, separate those people from me.

This means that the question of whether or not the kingdom continues to exist after death (apart from the fact that no one is capable of answering it) is somewhat moot. It is only as important, I would say, as our own narcissistic interest in ourselves. Indeed, I would suggest that people's spiritual elevation could be accurately measured by their greater or lesser indifference to the question of their own immortality. If we are already in the kingdom, we are already saved. What could death take away from us? What more could immortality give us?

Surprisingly enough, when Thomas Aquinas picked up the debate some nine centuries after Saint Augustine, he went even further. The gist of his thinking on the matter can be found in his *Summa Theologica* (2.1.65.5 and 2.2.18.2). The angelical doctor said much the same thing as Saint Augustine: in the kingdom, both faith and hope will have disappeared ('neither one of these can exist in the blessed'); all that will remain are charity and love. To this statement, however, he added something quite astonishing – something I have never come across in Saint Augustine or anywhere else, and which, I admit, gave me quite a shock when I first read it. 'In Christ,' Saint Thomas calmly wrote, 'there was perfect charity, but there was neither faith nor hope.'

Of course I realize that to Thomas Aquinas's mind, there was neither faith nor hope in Christ because Christ was God, and God needs neither to believe in God (since he knows himself) nor to hope for anything (since he is both omniscient and omnipotent); you can hope only for things you do not know, or things you are not certain of accomplishing. This is clarified later in the text: 'Christ had neither faith nor hope because these contain imperfection. But in the place of faith, he had direct vision; and in the place of hope, full comprehension. And thus it was that charity was perfect in him.'

Still, for the faithful atheist I try to be, this passage does give a particular significance – and a powerful one – to a famous book called *The Imitation of Our Lord Jesus Christ*. If Jesus himself, as even Saint Thomas acknowledged, was inhabited by neither faith nor hope, then being faithful to Jesus (and attempting, with the means at our disposal, to follow his example) would not entail imitating either his faith or his hope; it might entail imitating his vision and comprehension (as Christians do through faith and hope and as Spinoza does through philosophy); it would definitely entail imitating his love (such is the ethics of the Gospel – or, again, Spinoza's ethics).

I am well aware that a different interpretation of the Gospels is possible – and even, for most Christians, necessary.

Indeed, I agree with them that, had Jesus been truly human, he would have had to share our ignorance as well, and our finitude, and our anxiety, and thus also the concomitant faith and hope (specifically those of the pious Jewish community to which he belonged). He did experience sadness and anguish, exclaiming at Gethsemane, for instance, 'My soul is exceeding sorrowful, even unto death . . .'; how could he not have experienced hope as well? But our endeavour here is not one of critical interpretation. What touches and enlightens me in the passage from Saint Thomas, as already in Saint Augustine and Saint Paul, is that love is greater – that is, at once more divine and more human – than either faith or hope. In a word, while by no means denying everything that separates those who believe in heaven from those who do not, I am trying to find a point of intersection between the two groups and determine what might bring them together, where they might be able to meet and attempt, at least occasionally, to communicate.

Again, it all boils down to fidelity, but in this case less to what separates us than to what unites us, namely, the best that humanity has created. Who would refuse to acknowledge that this is what the Gospels represent? True, the same can be said of the Socratic tradition in Greece, Buddha in India and Lao-tzu or Confucius in China. So what? When summits are involved, why should we need to choose? When sources are involved, why should we need to exclude? The mind knows no fatherland, nor does humanity.

Intellectually, I often feel closer to Buddhism or Taoism (to say nothing of Chan, which is like a synthesis of the two) than to Christianity, if only because none of those three Eastern spiritualities posits the existence of God, which is always refreshing for an atheist. I find Buddha and Lao-tzu more convincing than Moses or Saint Paul; I would rather study Nagarjuna or Dōgen than Meister Eckehart or Saint Francis of Assisi. For all that, I am not planning to open an ashram in the centre of France, to start believing in reincarnation or to make decisions about my future based on the *I Ching* . . . Intellectual proximity isn't everything. There is also the fact of having been immersed in a particular society since childhood, having interiorized its language (and the mental structures that go along with it), its habits, traditions, myths, sensitivity and affectivity. History counts at least as much as intelligence, and geography more than genes. We are part of the Western world. This is an excellent reason not to forget the horrors our civilization has perpetrated (the Inquisition, slavery, colonialism, totalitarianism); it is also an excellent reason to preserve those of its inventions we deem precious and even irreplaceable. There are atheists all over the world, but Western atheists are probably quite different from Asian or African atheists. I am leery of exoticism, spiritual tourism, syncretism, New Age or fashionable Eastern confusionism. I prefer to delve more deeply into our own tradition, which is that of Socrates and Jesus – but also that of Epicurus and Spinoza, Montaigne and Kant –

and to see where that path, since it happens to be my own, can lead an atheist.

This is what authorizes me to address Christians more specifically (they are my family, given that my family was Christian; and they are my history, given that it is still going on) and to tell them: I feel separated from you by only *three days* – those which, according to tradition, separate Good Friday from Easter Sunday. For the faithful atheist I try to be (atheism is easy; fidelity far less so), a large part of the Gospels continues to be valid. If pressed, I could acknowledge virtually everything as true, apart from the good Lord. I say 'if pressed' because I do not tend to turn the other cheek when being aggressed upon. I say 'virtually' because I am no fan of miracles. Still, nonviolence is only a part of the Gospels' message, and it would need to be relativized by the others. Besides, how many people are interested in the Gospels primarily because of the miracles they describe? My friend and master Marcel Conche once told me that I attached too much importance to the evangelical tradition. It was too irrational, he said. He himself preferred the Greeks; he preferred philosophy; and here is how he put it: 'Your Jesus couldn't have had much confidence in his arguments if he had to resort to walking on water!' The quip gave me a good laugh – and certainly it rang true – but it bypasses the essentials of the Christian doctrine. I would gladly dispense with miracles, which of course I don't believe in, and many Christians agree when I say that they are not the most important part of the Gospels. Jesus is much more than a fakir or a magician. What matters in his message is love, not miracles.

This is why I find the story of his life, such as it has come down to us, so very touching and enlightening. The baby born in a stable; the child in flight for his life; the young boy engaging in debate with erudite church fathers; the young man flying into a fury at the temple merchants; the message of love that sums up the Law and the Prophets; the Sabbath being made for man and not man for the Sabbath; Jesus' acceptance or anticipation of the separation of church and state ('Render therefore unto Caesar the things which are Caesar's'); his sense of universal humanity ('Inasmuch as ye have done it unto one of the least of these, ye have done it unto me'); his valuing of the present moment ('Take therefore no thought for the morrow, for the morrow shall take thought for the things of itself'); his freedom of spirit ('the truth shall make you free'); the parables of the Good Samaritan, the young rich man and the prodigal son; the Sermon on the Mount ('Blessed are the meek . . . they which do hunger and thirst after righteousness . . . the peacemakers . . .'); Jesus' solitude (on Mount Olivet, for instance); his courage; his humiliation; his crucifixion . . . The story is enough to move anyone. You might say that I have forged a sort of inner Christ for myself – one who is indeed 'meek and lowly in heart' but who is purely human, who guides me and keeps me company. What I cannot believe is that he took himself for God. His life and message move me all the more, but for me the story ends with Jesus nailed to the cross at Calvary, quoting the Psalmist as he sobs, 'My God, my God, why hast thou forsaken me?' He is truly our brother at that moment, for he shares our distress and anguish, our suffering and solitude, our despair.

For believers, the story does not end there but goes on three more days (until the Resurrection) or as many as forty more (until the Ascension). I am well aware that through the Resurrection, those days open on to eternity; this is an important difference indeed, and I am by no means trying to efface it. Still, is it reasonable to lend more importance to the few days that separate us than to the thirty-three preceding years, which – in their human content, at least – bring us together?

If Jesus did not rise from the dead, does this make his murderers right? Does it render his message of love and justice null and void? Of course not. Thus, the most important thing – not salvation but 'the truth and the life' – is preserved.

Is there life after death? No one can say. Most Christians believe there is. I do not. There is life *before* death, however. On that much we can agree, at least!

Let us sum up what has been said so far. It is possible to do without religion but not without communion, fidelity or love. In these matters, what we share is more important than what separates us. Peace to all, believers and unbelievers alike. Life is more precious than religion; this is where inquisitors and torturers are wrong. Communion is more precious than churches; this is where sectarians are wrong. Finally – and this is where fine people are right, whether they believe in God or not – love is more precious than hope or despair.

There is no need to wait until we are saved to be human.

Chapter II

Does God Exist?

Now comes the hardest part, or at least the most uncertain. Where God is concerned, two questions need to be raised: that of his definition and that of his existence. No science, now or ever, can answer these questions. This is no reason to renounce thinking about them. No science can tell us how to live and die, either, but this is no reason to be indifferent to how we live and die.

A Preliminary Definition

What is God? No one can say. He is reputed to be ungraspable, ineffable, incomprehensible. That difficulty shouldn't daunt us, however. Though we cannot know what God *is*, we can specify what we mean when we use the word that refers to him. Though we cannot give the word a *real* definition, as the scholastics used to say, we can and should try to give it a *nominal* definition. It may be only a starting point, but it is indispensable. If we don't have a preliminary definition of what God is, how can we answer – or even seriously formulate – the question of whether or not he exists? How can we discuss the matter if we don't know what it is we're discussing?

'Do you believe in God, Professor?' Thus interrogated by a journalist, Einstein answered simply, 'First tell me what you mean by God, and then I'll tell you if I believe in him.' That is the correct procedure. A nominal definition is necessary for believers and atheists alike; both should know just what it is they do or do not believe in. It is also – for the moment, at least – sufficient.

Given the fact that, as noted at the outset, I function within a monotheistic framework, and more specifically within the framework of Western philosophy, I would propose the following definition of God. It is by no means original (if it were, it would be bad); its only purpose is to allow us to agree on the object of debate. By *God*, I mean an eternal, spiritual and transcendent being, both exterior and superior to nature, who consciously and voluntarily created the universe. He is assumed to be perfect and blessed, omniscient and omnipotent. Infinitely kind and just, the Creator, being his own cause, is himself uncreated. He is the Supreme Being upon whom everything depends and who himself depends on nothing. He is the enactment and the personification of the absolute.

This nominal definition clarifies the meaning of our second question – that of God's existence – to which we shall devote considerably more time. No science, it should be repeated, can answer this question – nor can any form of knowledge (if by knowledge we mean, as we should, the communicable and repeatable result of a demonstration or an experience). Does God exist? We do not know. We never shall know, at least not in this life – hence the question of whether to believe in him or not. For my part, I do not; I'm an atheist. Why? This is what I shall attempt to explain in the following pages.

Atheism or Agnosticism?

I have no proof. No one does. I do, however, have a certain number of reasons or arguments that seem to me stronger than the ones which make the opposite case. I am what you might call a nondogmatic atheist – that is, I do not claim to *know* that God does not exist, but I *believe* he does not exist.

'In that case,' people sometimes object, 'you're not an atheist but an agnostic.' This is worth a few words of explanation. Agnostics and atheists do have something in common, namely the fact that they do not believe in God. This is why people often confuse them. Atheists go further, however – they believe that God does not exist. Agnostics believe neither that God exists nor that he does not exist. Agnosticism is like a negative atheism, or an atheism by default. Agnostics do not deny the existence of God, as atheists do; rather, they leave the question up in the air.

Etymologies in this area can be misleading, *Agnōstos*, in Greek, means the unknown or unknowable. People often conclude that agnostics are those who acknowledge their ignorance on the subject of God or the absolute. But who can deny it? Were we to accept this definition, everyone would be agnostic except the most headstrong among us, and agnosticism would lose in comprehensibility what it gained in applicability. It would be less a particular position than a general characteristic of the human condition. Such is not the case. No one *knows*, in the strongest sense of the word, whether or not God exists. Believers say he does; this is what is known as a profession of faith. Atheists say he does not. Agnostics neither affirm nor deny his existence; they refuse to make up their minds, or claim to be incapable of doing so.

'Well, then, I must be an idiot,' a friend recently retorted, 'because I'm convinced that God does not exist.' This is conflating conviction and knowledge. What is the difference between the two? Kant answered this question in his *Critique of Pure Reason*. He distinguished among three degrees of belief and assent: *opinion*, which admits that it is both subjectively and objectively insufficient, *faith*, which is subjectively but not objectively sufficient, and finally, *knowledge*, which is both subjectively and objectively sufficient. Though our vocabularies may differ (where atheists are concerned, I prefer the word *conviction* – which Kant also uses on occasion – to the word *faith*, whose connotations are too specifically religious), the distinction seems to me a useful one. My friend's atheism is a conviction, whereas mine is closer to an opinion. Similarly, some believers have religious convictions (i.e., faith), whereas others, less sure of themselves or of God, are content with having religious opinions. But on the subject of God's existence, what intelligent and lucid person could claim to have knowledge, that is, a subjectively *and objectively* sufficient credence? If such a thing was possible, then that person should be able to convince us, for it is in the nature of knowledge to be transmittable to any normally intelligent and cultivated individual, and atheism would long ago have vanished. The least that can be said is that such is not the case.

'Will atheists still exist fifty years from now?' a journalist once asked me. Of course they will. His asking me the question, however, is revelatory of a change in cultural climate. In my youth, we were more inclined to wonder whether believers would still exist in the twenty-first century. The return of religiosity, though not of equal intensity all over the planet, is one of the most salient features of our time. This obviously proves nothing, apart from the fact that the question remains open, as it has for the past three millennia. There is no reason that this should change. Over and above intellectual fashions and opinion trends, everything seems to suggest that religion and irreligion are destined to live together for a long time to come. This is not necessarily a problem. Only sectarians and fanatics should be bothered by it. Among the world's greatest intellectuals, some (even in America) are atheists; others (even in Europe) are believers. This proves only that no knowledge, either today or yesterday, has come along to decide between them.

The most appropriate attitude would seem to be not agnosticism but tolerance and open-mindedness. The truth is that no one knows whether or not God exists and that many, among believers and atheists alike, are willing to acknowledge their irreducible unknowingness, which is humanity's destiny. This is what makes metaphysics so attractive and occasionally so exhilarating. If you derive no pleasure from it, the least you can do is refrain from spoiling other people's pleasure.

Some believers will object that they do not consider themselves unknowing: God has given them the truth once and for all. Revelation is enough for them; why would they need proofs, arguments or reasons? They throw themselves into the study of the Book, committing it to memory and reciting it ceaselessly. How can we object to that, except by saying that revelation is valid only for those who believe in it and thus cannot be used, unless you enjoy vicious circles, to found the very faith that validates it?

Indeed, what sort of revelation do they mean? The Bible? With or without the New Testament? The Koran? The Vedas? The Avesta? Why not the Raelian mumbo-jumbo? There are any number of religions. How choose among them? How does one reconcile them? Their disciples – even under the auspices of the same revelation – have been squabbling for centuries (the Catholic church against first the Orthodox church, then the Cathars, then the Protestants; the Shia against the Sunnis; and so forth). So many deaths – all in the name of the same Book! So many massacres – all in the name of the same God! Proof enough that all of us are in a state of nonknowledge. People do not murder one another for mathematics, or for any other science – nor even for any true fact, once its truth has been established. They murder each other only for the sake of what they do not know, or what they are unable to prove. Thus, religious wars are a powerful argument against all forms of religious dogmatism. They prove the latter to be not only extremely dangerous (because of the hatred and atrocities to which it gives rise) but also extremely weak, for had any one of these religions been able to advance the least proof, it would not have needed to exterminate the others. 'It is putting a very high price on one's conjectures,' as Montaigne expressed it, 'to have a man roasted alive because of them.' But no one would burn a man alive for a demonstrable truth. Hence, no matter what their proponents believe, the Inquisition, the Crusades and the Jihad tend to reinforce the very doubt they set out to destroy. The horror they unleash tends to confirm the fact that no one has true knowledge where God is concerned. Thus, we are doomed to either religious wars or tolerance, according to whether passion or lucidity carry the day.

This by no means implies that we should renounce having an opinion. Tolerance does not preclude reflection. Uncertainty does not preclude choice; on the contrary, rigorously speaking, choice can occur only where there is uncertainty. Philosophy means thinking beyond the knowable. Metaphysics means thinking as far as possible. This is where we encounter the question of God – and the possibility, for each of us, to try to answer it.

Agnostics, not content with admitting they don't know what to think about the absolute (many believers and unbelievers are prepared to admit as much), stop there and refuse to go any further. They prefer not to take sides on the subject of what they do not know. Ultimately, then, they defend a sort of neutrality, scepticism or indifference regarding religious matters. This attitude dates back at least as far as Protagoras, and is certainly worthy of respect: 'Of the gods, I can say nothing – neither that they are, nor that they are not, nor what they are. Too many things prevent me from knowing: firstly the vagueness of the question and secondly the brevity of human life.' In the great metaphysical opinion poll, in other words, agnostics tick the 'no opinion' box. Such is not my case at all! I am fully prepared to acknowledge my ignorance, which is the same as that of every other human being. On the other hand, I care as much as any believer about defending my opinion, my choice – my 'bet', as Pascal would say (though, as will soon be seen, my bet doesn't come down on the same side as his). I am neither neutral nor indifferent. Am I sceptical? Partly. Suffice it to say that I admit to having no proofs. Again, I am a nondogmatic atheist, but that by no means implies that I am without convictions or beliefs.

'People who believe they have the truth,' as Jules Lequier put it, 'should know they believe it, rather than believe they know it.' This is where I stand, particularly as regards religion. I don't *know* whether God exists or not, but I know I *believe* he doesn't! Though atheism is a negative belief (*atheos*, in Greek, means 'without God'), it is still a belief – that is, less than a certainty, but far more than the mere admission of unknowing or the cautious or comfortable refusal to make up one's mind. Thus – allow me to insist – I am an atheist, not an agnostic. 'We are on board,' to quote Pascal once again. The question of God is put to us by our finite nature, our angst, our history, our civilization, our intelligence – and, yes, by our ignorance as well. I can't claim to take no interest in it or feign to have no opinion on the subject. Being a nondogmatic atheist makes me no less of an atheist! It only makes me, I hope, more lucid.

What Is Dangerous, Religion or Fanaticism?

Why do I not believe in God? For any number of reasons, not all of which are rational. In matters such as these, many factors enter into play: sensitivity (yes, there is such a thing as metaphysical sensitivity), personal history, imagination, culture – perhaps grace as well, for those who believe in it, or the unconscious. Who can measure the influence of family and friends on our religious convictions, to say nothing of the period we live in? However, the nature of the present book being not autobiographical but philosophical, I hope I shall be forgiven for sticking to rational arguments. Even there, after twenty-five centuries of philosophizing, the potential list is virtually inexhaustible on both sides. Not being a historian, and not wishing to write a thick book, I shall content myself with six main arguments – those that seem to me the most powerful or that I personally find the most convincing.

I shall deliberately leave aside everything that might be held against religions or churches, which, admittedly, are always imperfect, often despicable, and sometimes criminal, but whose defects have nothing to do with the issue at hand. The Inquisition, for example, or Islamic terrorism, clearly prove beyond the shadow of a doubt that religion can be dangerous, but they prove nothing as to the existence of God. By definition, all religions are human. The fact that they all have blood on their hands could justifiably turn me into a misanthrope, but it is not an argument in favour of atheism – which, indeed, has itself committed a fair number of crimes, particularly in the twentieth century.

What incites people to commit massacres is not faith; it is fanaticism, whether religious or political. It is intolerance. It is hatred. Believing in God can be dangerous. We need only remember the massacre of Saint Bartholomew's Day, the Crusades, the wars of religion, the Jihad, the September 11 attacks . . . Not believing in God can be equally dangerous. We need only remember Stalin, Mao Tse-tung or Pol Pot . . . Who will add up the deaths on either side and decide what they mean? Horror is numberless, with or without God. Alas, this tells us more about humanity than it does about religion.

Moreover, among believers and unbelievers alike, there

have been brave heroes, extraordinary artists and thinkers, marvellous individuals. To condemn their beliefs out of hand would be to betray them. I have too much admiration for Pascal and Leibniz, Bach and Tolstoy – to say nothing of Gandhi, Etty Hillesum or Martin Luther King, Jr – to turn up my nose at the faith that inspired them. And I have too much affection for the believers among my loved ones to wish to offend them in any way. Disagreement among friends can be healthy, joyful and stimulating; condescension and contempt cannot.

Moreover, I have little taste for pamphleteering and polemics. What matters is what is true, not what is victorious, and the subject I wish to discuss in this chapter is God, not his henchmen or his zealots. So it is time we got round to him – or, rather, to my reasons for not believing in him.

Weakness of the Proofs

My first three arguments will be essentially negative ones, that is, they are reasons more in favour of atheism than against piety.

The first, since we must begin somewhere, is the weakness of the opposing arguments, and in particular the so-called proofs of God's existence. I prefer not to spend a great deal of time on these proofs (philosophers, including pious philosophers, long ago renounced trying to prove the existence of God), but I cannot remain completely silent on the subject. The three most important ones, those most often referred to by the tradition, must be mentioned at least briefly – namely, the ontological proof, the cosmological proof and the physico-theological proof.

The Ontological Proof

The first argument is the most disconcerting one. It is thought to have been first advanced in the eleventh century by Saint Anselm of Canterbury, but it has recurred (under various guises) in the writings of Descartes, Spinoza, Leibniz and Hegel. It purports to show that God exists by definition, i.e., that his existence is indissociable from his essence. It does so through an exercise (or an artifice?) of pure logic, which derives nothing at all from experience (hence the fact that this argument is sometimes called the a-priori proof). Its substance is disarmingly simple. You begin, quite classically, by defining God as the supreme being, 'a being such that no greater one can be conceived', as Saint Anselm puts it; this being is utterly perfect (Descartes, Leibniz) or absolutely infinite (Spinoza, Hegel). Such is the traditional, almost banal definition of God. Yet for the proponents of the ontological proof, its consequences are far reaching indeed. If God did not exist, he would be neither the greatest nor truly infinite, and his perfection would be lacking something (to say the least). Now, this is contrary to his definition. Therefore, God exists by definition – or, as is claimed to amount to the same thing – by essence. To think about God – to conceive of him as supreme, perfect infinite – is to think of him as existing. What about atheists? They think wrongly, or do not know what they think. To conceive of 'God without existence', explains Descartes, is to contradict oneself – it is tantamount to conceiving 'a supremely perfect Being devoid of a supreme perfection'. It follows that 'existence is inseparable from Him, and hence that He really exists'. The concept of God, as Hegel was later to say, 'includes being'; God is the only entity who exists by his very essence.

This is an astonishing, fascinating, infuriating proof indeed. I have no idea if it ever convinced anyone. Anselm, who was Archbishop of Canterbury, was a believer long before he invented it. In any case, it convinced neither Brother Gaunilo – a contemporary of Anselm's and, like him, a Benedictine monk – nor Thomas Aquinas; both would write in-depth critiques of the notion. Nor did it convince Pascal, Pierre Gassendi, Hume or Kant – to say nothing of Diderot, Nietzsche, Gottlob Frege or Bertrand Russell! It is a strange proof, indeed, that convinces only the already convinced! How could a definition possibly prove an existence? One might just as well try to get rich by defining wealth. Such, in substance, was Gaunilo's objection as far back as the eleventh century. Such was to be Kant's objection seven centuries later, and it is a decisive one. Being is neither a supplementary perfection, as Descartes claims it to be, nor a true predicate – it adds nothing to a concept, nor can it be deduced from it. This is why it is always illegitimate to extrapolate from concept to existence: a thousand real dollars contain nothing more, as Kant's argument shows, than a thousand possible dollars (the concept is the same in both cases). Still, I am far better off with a thousand real dollars 'than with their mere concept or possibility'. The same is true of God. The concept of God remains the same whether God exists or not; thus, it cannot be used to prove that God exists.

In a word, this 'proof' is anything but a proof. And given the fact that, as Kant shows, all the other proofs boil down to it, since all of them assume that we can extrapolate from concept to existence, there can be no proof of the existence of God. God's existence can only be postulated, not demonstrated. It is an object of faith, not knowledge. In so saying Kant was siding with Pascal against Descartes and with Hume against Saint Anselm. The a-priori proof would never recover. Despite Hegel's valiant efforts, the ontological argument is a thing of the past, not the future. If it continues to shine, and then even dazzles on occasion, it is more as a monument to the human spirit than as a proof of God's existence. Indeed, even if this argument proved the existence of an absolutely infinite being (as Hegel claimed it did), how could we be certain this being was God? It might also be Nature, as Spinoza believed – that is, a being that, though indeed infinite, is immanent and impersonal, will-less, goal-less, improvident and unloving . . . I doubt that our believers could content themselves with that.

The Cosmological Proof
The same objection could be raised for the cosmological proof, also known as the proof *a contingentia mundi* ('by the contingency of the universe'). Let us first introduce it briefly,

as it is found, for instance, in Leibniz, who doubtless gave it its most powerful and succinct formulation. It is an a-posteriori rather than an a-priori proof. Its starting point is an experiential fact, namely the existence of the universe. Like all facts, it must have an explanation, by virtue of what Leibniz calls the principle of sufficient reason, i.e., nothing exists or is true without a cause or a reason. Now, the universe is incapable of explaining itself: its existence is not necessary but contingent (it could have *not* existed). Thus, it must have a cause or a 'sufficient reason' other than itself. What could that be? Were the cause itself contingent, it would need to be explained by another cause, which would in turn need to be explained by another cause, which would in turn need to be explained by a third, and so on and so forth; this would end up leaving the entire series of contingent phenomena, and thus the existence of the universe, unexplained. To satisfy the principle of sufficient reason, it is necessary, as Aristotle pointed out, to stop somewhere. This does not leave us much choice: we can escape from the endless regression only by positing as a sufficient reason for the universe the existence of a being that does not itself need another reason – that is, an absolutely necessary being, one that cannot *not* exist – one that, as Leibniz puts it, carries 'its own reason for existing with it'. In a word, the set of contingent things (the universe) can be explained only by an absolutely necessary being located outside of itself; and that being, or 'ultimate reason for things', is what is known as God.

Of the three classical 'proofs' of God's existence, this is the only one I find powerful, the only one that occasionally makes me vacillate or hesitate. Why? Because contingency is an abyss in which reason loses its bearings. Disorientation, however, does not constitute a proof. Why shouldn't reason – our reason – get lost in the universe, if the latter is too big, too deep, too complex, too dark or too bright for it? Indeed, how can we be certain our reason is perfectly rational? Only a God could guarantee us that, and this is just what prevents our reason from proving his existence. It would be a vicious circle, as it is in Descartes: our reason proves the existence of God, and God guarantees the veracity of our reason. 'To the greater glory of Pyrrhonism', as Pascal would say. That our reason stumbles and feels dizzy when confronted with the abyss of contingency proves that we would like to get to the bottom of the abyss, not that the abyss has a bottom.

Let us approach this from a different angle. The crux of the cosmological proof is the principle of sufficient reason, which claims that all facts are brought into existence by some cause. Why the universe? Because God. This is the realm of causes. Why God? Because the universe. This is the realm of reasons. But how do we know there *is* an order? How do we know reason is right? What makes us think there is no such thing as the absolutely inexplicable? Why should contingency not have the last word – or the final silence? Because it would be absurd? So what? Why shouldn't the truth be absurd? Actually, it would be not so much absurd as mysterious, and for any finite spirit, the truth of the universe must indeed be mysterious. How can we expect to understand and explain everything, given the fact that the 'everything' was here long before we were, and formed us, and permeates our very being, and surpasses us in every direction? One does not need much lucidity to grasp the fact that being is a mystery. How could we possibly explain its existence, given that all forms of explanation depend upon it?

Even were we to agree with Leibniz and the principle of reason, this would prove neither more nor less than the existence of a necessary being. But how could we be certain it was God – *id est*, a Spirit, a Subject and a Person (or three people)? It could equally be Anaximander's *apeiron* (the infinite, the undetermined), Heraclitus's ever-changing fire (becoming), Parmenides' impersonal Being, Lao-tzu's equally impersonal Tao . . . It could also be what Spinoza called Substance, namely that which is its own cause and the cause of everything else, which is absolutely necessary, eternal and infinite – but immanent (whose effects are within itself) and devoid, as we pointed out for the ontological proof, of any and all anthropomorphic traits, having neither conscience, will nor love. True, Spinoza called this 'God', but it is definitely not 'the good Lord'; it is neither more nor less than Nature (this is what is referred to as Spinoza's pantheism): '*Deus sive Natura*, God, which is to say Nature'. As such, it is not a subject and pursues no goal. Why pray to it, since it is not listening to us? Why obey it, since it has given us no orders? Why trust it, since it takes no interest in us? And in that case, what remains of faith? Leibniz was right. This form of pantheism is closer to atheism than it is to religion.

That there is such a thing as being is not open to debate. And that being is necessary is also something I am inclined to believe (it is my 'Spinozist' side). Might the universe not have been? Yes, but only for the imagination, and only as long as it was not (as is suggested by the unreal tense of the question: *might have*) – not for itself and for what it is. In the present, reality knows only the indicative, or, rather, the present indicative is the only tense of reality, which makes it necessary by definition. Because everything is predetermined? No, because everything *is* and cannot (in the present) be other than what it is. The principle of identity is sufficient: what is cannot not be, since it is. Such is the true (and perhaps the only) principle of reason. What about the possible? Either it is real or it is not. Contingency is neither more nor less than the shadow cast by nothingness, or imagined reality (what did not come into being, what might have been), within the vast space of being and becoming (what was, is, and shall be). To put it succinctly, as we must, it could be said that contingency is conceivable only *sub specie temporis* (from the point of view of time), that necessity is conceivable only *sub specie aeternitatis* (from the point of view of eternity) and that, taken together in the present, the two are impossible to distinguish. The same, I think, could be said of mystery and fact.

The Mystery of Being

'I'm not an atheist,' a friend of mine said recently. 'I believe there is something . . . an energy . . .' Ha, no kidding! I, too, believe there is something, an energy. This, indeed, is exactly what physicists teach us: being is energy. But to believe in God is not to believe in an energy; it is to believe in a will, or a love! It is not to believe in something; it is to believe in Someone! And *that* – that will, that love, that Someone – the God of Abraham and Jacob, the God of Jesus or the God of Muhammad – is what I personally do not believe in.

That there is 'something' is not open to doubt. And that this 'something' is a force of some kind (what the Greeks called *energeia*, what Spinoza called *conatus*, what modern physics calls energy) is self-evident to anyone capable of observing nature. The question is not *whether* but *why* there is something. Why nature? Why energy? Why being? Why becoming? This was Leibniz's great question: 'Why is there something rather than nothing?' It is a question that goes beyond God, since it includes him. Why is there God rather than nothing? The question of being is primordial and recurs constantly. Yet no one can answer it. To say that being is eternal is not to explain it: that there has always been being relieves us of having to search for its commencement or its origin, not of having to search for its explanation. To think of being as necessary is not to explain it either; it is merely to recognize that it can be explained only by itself (it is 'its own cause', as the philosophers often put it), which makes it forever inexplicable to us.

Philosophers are as much at the mercy of this mystery as physicists and theologians. Why the Big Bang rather than nothing? Why God rather than nothing? Why everything rather than nothing? The question 'Why is there something rather than nothing?' is all the more necessary for being unanswerable. It is all the more fascinating, enlightening, stimulating because it confronts us with the mystery of being, which is indissociable from its self-evidence. It startles us out of our positivistic sleep. It upsets our habits, our familiarities and our so-called obvious facts. It detaches us, at least temporarily, from the apparent banality and normalcy of reality. It sends us back to our original astonishment: there is something, not nothing! And no one will ever be able to say why, given that the existence of being could be explained only by entities that *are* – in other words, we would need to assume what we are attempting to explain. Thus, the existence of being is intrinsically mysterious. *This* is what needs to be understood – this, and the fact that the mystery is irreducible. Not because it is impenetrable but (on the contrary) because we are inside it. Not because it is too dark, but because it is light itself.

The Physico-Theological Proof
The ontological proof proves nothing. The cosmological proof proves, at most, the existence of a necessary being

but not that of a spiritual or personal God. This may be why a third 'proof', known as the physico-theological proof, has been so popular over the past twenty-five centuries. Of all the proofs, it is the simplest, the most obvious . . . and the most debatable. It dates back at least as far as Plato, the Stoics and Cicero. It can be found in Nicolas de Malebranche, François Fénelon, Leibniz, Voltaire, Rousseau . . . It is an a-posteriori proof based on the notions of order and finality, which is why I sometimes refer to it as the physico-*teleological* proof, from the Greek *telos*, end or goal. Its reasoning is simple, almost naïvely so. You start out by observing the world; you note that there is order in the world, order of daunting complexity; and you conclude that there must be an ordering intelligence. This is what, today, is known as the theory of intelligent design. The world, it claims, is too well ordered, too complex, too beautiful, too harmonious to be the result of mere chance; at the origin of such extraordinary beauty and complexity there can only be a creative, ordering intelligence, which must be God.

The least that can be said about this argument is that it is not new. Cicero formulated it in *De natura deorum*. Voltaire, who was both a freethinker and a deist, revived it: 'All works that display both means and an end presuppose a workman; therefore this universe, made up of moving forces, of means each of which has its end, presupposes a highly powerful and intelligent workman.' Voltaire expressed the same notion in a famous couplet:

The universe impresses me; I cannot help but balk
To think that there should be no clockmaker for
  such a clock.

The clock argument, a traditional one, must be taken
seriously. It is merely an analogy, of course, but it is a striking one. Imagine that one of our astronauts were to
stumble upon a watch while exploring an apparently unin-
habited planet. No one could suggest that such a complex
mechanism was the result of mere chance; we would all be
convinced that the watch had been made by a being gifted
with intelligence and will. Now, the universe, or any one of
its parts (the smallest flower, the tiniest insect, any one of
our organs) is far more complex than the most complex
watch; thus, at least as much as in the case of the watch if
not more so, we must assume that they were intentionally
created by an intelligent being, one who – since we are trying to explain the entire universe – can only be God.

Despite its suggestiveness, the analogy has a number of
weaknesses. Firstly, it is only an analogy; the universe is
clearly *not* made up of springs and gears. Secondly – more
on this later – it makes short shrift of the countless examples of *disorder*, horror and dysfunction in the universe. A
cancerous tumour can also be described as a kind of clock
(as in a time bomb); an earthquake, if we wish to prolong
the clockwork metaphor, would be something like a plan-
etary buzzer or alarm. Does this prove that tumours
and cataclysms are all part of an intelligent, benevolent

design? Thirdly and most importantly, the analogy advanced by Voltaire and Rousseau is out of date. Its model (like eighteenth-century physics) is mechanical, whereas nature as described by contemporary science has more to do with dynamics (being is energy), randomness (Nature plays dice – this is just what distinguishes it from God) and general entropy (what would we think of a clock that tended towards maximal disorder?). It is true that life cre ates order, complexity and meaning. But the negative entropy of all living things, apart from the fact that life is a spatially and temporally circumscribed phenomenon (on Earth, it will not survive the disappearance of the Sun), has grown increasingly comprehensible since Darwin: being a far simpler hypothesis, the evolution of species and natural selection can advantageously replace the providential plans of a mysterious Creator. This is why the proponents of 'intelligent design' so often attack Darwinism, sometimes going so far as to suggest – in the name of the Bible! – that it should no longer be taught in schools, or else taught alongside Genesis. If randomness (of mutations) leads to order (through natural selection), then God is no longer needed to explain the appearance of man. Nature suffices. This is not proof that God does not exist, but it does take an argument away from believers.

We must beware of analogies. Life is undeniably more complex than a clock, but it is also more fertile (have you ever seen a clock give birth to other clocks?), more evolu- tive, more selective and more creative. That changes everything! Were we to find a wristwatch on a hitherto unexplored planet, no one could deny it was the result of willed, intelligent action. On the other hand, were we to find a bacterium, a flower or an animal, no scientist – not even one who believed in God – would doubt that this living thing, no matter how complex, was the result of natural laws. It might be objected that this does not explain the existence of those laws themselves. Of course it doesn't. This is why the existence of God remains as conceivable as his inexistence – but not more so. Still, the physico-theological proof has suffered greatly from scientific progress. We are increasingly knowledgeable about order and apparent finality (the movement of the planets, the teleonomy of living beings) and increasingly aware of disorder and chance. When the sun goes out, some five billion years from now, the physico-theological proof will probably lose most of its advocates. Either that, or they will be in heaven by then. Though the alternative remains open, it does seem to indicate that this 'proof' is not really a proof at all.

The Absence of Proof: A Reason to Not Believe

Other 'proofs' have been advanced, of course, but virtually all of them can be reduced to one or the other of the three just discussed. Such is the case, to take a famous example, for Thomas Aquinas's five 'paths', which attempt to extrapolate God's existence from its effects. The first three paths – namely, *movement*, which, as in Aristotle, takes us back to a *primum mobile*; *effective cause*, which, as in Avicenna, takes us back to a first cause; and *through the possible*, which takes us back to an absolutely necessary Being – are akin to the cosmological proof. The fourth path – *the degrees of existence*, which takes us back to a supreme Being – though a posteriori, has much in common with Saint Anselm's argument. Finally, the fifth path – the *ultimate cause*, which takes us back to an ordering Intelligence – is no more nor less than a formulation of the physico-theological argument.

As for Descartes, it is well known that he was dissatisfied with the ontological proof. In his third *Meditation on First Philosophy* (whereas he would not spell out the ontological argument until the fifth), he also set forth a number of proofs by effects that could be assimilated neither to the cosmological proof nor to Aquinas's paths. Here, God's existence was inferred not from the existence of the world (which, at this point in his demonstration, Descartes still considered dubious) but, as only the *Cogito* can permit, from the existence within himself of the idea of God as infinite substance (first proof by effects) or from his own existence in so far as it possessed this idea (second proof by effects). Descartes himself acknowledged that these two proofs were essentially one and the same: I find within myself the idea of God as an infinite and perfect Being; like all other things, this idea must have a cause; since 'there must be at least as much reality in the cause as in its effect', the cause itself must be infinite and perfect; it can be none other than God.

This argument convinces me even less than the onto-logical argument. Firstly, as already stated, nothing proves that the said infinite cause is a Subject or a Spirit (unless, that is, the idea of perfection itself presupposes it, which is anything but self-evident); it could just as well be Nature. Secondly, it is quite inaccurate to state that cause must be at least as real as its effects. Atoms cannot think, yet they are the cause of all the thoughts that teem in our brains. Finally, and most important, in human beings the idea of the infinite is a finite idea, just as the idea of per-fection is an imperfect one. We could almost go so far as to call this a defining trait of humankind. What is a human being? – a creature who (unlike God) is finite but who (unlike animals) can conceive of infinity, an imperfect crea-ture who possesses an idea of perfection. Just *because* we are human, our ideas of infinity and perfection are finite and imperfect. Otherwise, how could we think them? Man is a finite being who opens on to infinity, an imperfect being who dreams of perfection. This is what we call mind, and mind is all the greater for being aware of its own finite nature. Thus, Descartes's proof is inoperative. Once the finite nature of the idea of infinity within us has been acknowledged, the brain suffices to explain it; the brain can very well be the mind's potential, just as the mind is the brain's actualization. Humankind is at once finite and great; the body is finite, and the mind contains greatness.

What conclusions can be drawn from all of this? That there is – and can be – no such thing as a proof of the existence of God. Unfortunately for those who appreciate dogma, metaphysics is not a science; theology even less so; and no science can take their place. This is because no science can attain the absolute – at least, none can attain it absolutely. God is not a theorem. He is not something one can prove or demonstrate; he is something one can believe in – or not.

It might be objected that there is no proof that God does not exist, either. I quite readily admit this. However, it is rather less disturbing for atheism than it is for religion – not only because the burden of proof, as the saying goes, is on those who claim something exists but also because, on the scale of infinity, it is at most possible to prove what exists and impossible to prove what does not. By definition, nothingness produces no effects. How could it be anything but without proofs? True, with a bit of luck, I can prove that I did not commit a particular crime of which I am accused; all I need do is demonstrate its impossibility – by proving, for instance, that I was a thousand miles away when the dastardly deed was done. This is what is known as having an alibi. One outside witness suffices. However, there is no possible alibi for nothingness; there are no outside witnesses for the Great All. How would one go about proving the nonexistence of something? Try, for instance, to prove the nonexistence of Santa Claus, or vampires, or fairies or werewolves . . . You will not succeed. This is no reason to believe in them. On the other hand, the fact that no one has ever been able to prove their existence is a powerful reason *not* to believe in them. The same is true, *mutatis mutandis*, for the question at hand, though the stakes are admittedly higher and the improbability lower: the lack of proof of God's existence is an argument against any and all theistic religions. While this may not yet be a sufficient reason to be an atheist, it is at least a reason not to be a believer.

The Weakness of the Evidence

Thus the proofs are weak, since they do not exist. But the evidence, too – the evidence especially – is weak. This is my second argument, also a negative one. It is more important to me than the first. Where facts are concerned, experience is more crucial than reasoning.

One of my main reasons for not believing in God is that I have seen no evidence of his existence. This is the simplest argument of all, and one of the most powerful. I cannot help thinking that if God existed, he should be easier to perceive or feel. All you would need to do is open your eyes, or your soul. I keep trying to do this. And no matter how wide I open them, what I see is the world and what I love is humanity.

Most theologians, and some philosophers as well, go to great lengths to convince us that God exists. This is very kind of them. But it would be so much simpler and so much more effective if he would just appear to us! This is always the first objection that comes to mind when believers try to convert me. 'Why go to so much trouble?' I feel like asking them. 'If God wanted me to believe, it would be a cinch! If he doesn't want me to, why should you bother converting me?'

Of course, I am aware that believers since Isaiah have been talking about *Deus absconditus*, 'a God who conceals himself'. Some see his concealment as yet another of his qualities, a sort of divine discretion or supernatural tact, all the more admirable in that it protects us from the most beautiful, astonishing, dazzling sight of all! I cannot agree. Indeed, I find the idea of a stubbornly hiding God very surprising. If I believed in him, it would seem to me not so much tactful as childish, not so much discreet as dissembling. I'm too old for hide-and-seek or blindman's buff. The world and real life are far more interesting to me.

The notion of a hidden God can be found in the strongest strands of our tradition, from the kabbalah and Saint Augustine to Luther and Pascal. All I'm doing is trying to understand it. We can take the anthropomorphic metaphor a little further. Apart from when they are playing games, human beings hide only when frightened or ashamed. God's omnipotence precludes fear; his perfection precludes shame. So why should he feel the need to conceal himself? Does he want to surprise us? Does he think it's funny? That would be playing with our distress. 'My God, my God, why hast thou forsaken me?' The person who said that is our brother in pain. But what about the one who went on hiding while his son was being crucified? What God could possibly get a kick out of that?

We can now drop the metaphor and come to the crux of the question. Though said to be ubiquitous, God is invisible. Since he is reputed to be all-powerful, this means that he refuses to show himself. Why?

The answer most often advanced by believers is that God conceals himself so as to respect our freedom, or even to make it possible. Were he to manifest himself in his full glory, we are told, we would no longer have the choice of whether to believe in him or not. Faith would impose itself, or rather it would no longer be faith, since belief would be self-evident. What, in that case, would remain of our freedom? Nothing, explained Kant in his *Critique of Practical Reason*, and our morals would not survive such an event. Were God 'constantly before our eyes', or were we even able to prove his existence, which amounts to the same thing, our certainty would condemn us to what Kant calls heteronomy: in other words, in our own self-interest, we would have no choice but to submit. We would believe not out of moral excellence but out of caution. True, we might go on obeying the commandments, and moral law might be factually respected, but only out of self-interest. 'Most actions in conformity with the law would be produced by fear, only a few by hope, and none by duty.' Thus, Kant concludes, 'The moral value of our actions would no longer exist.' We would be the 'puppets' of egotism, jerked around by the strings of hope (of reward) and fear (of punishment) but utterly without freedom. Conversely, thanks to the fact that God conceals himself or that his existence remains uncertain, we are free to believe in him or not – and thus also free, according to Kant, to perform or not perform our duty.

This hypothesis seems to me a weak one, for three reasons.

Firstly, if God concealed himself in order to make us free – in other words, if ignorance is the condition of our freedom – this would imply that we are freer than God himself, since, unlike us, he does not have the choice of believing or not believing in his own existence! We would also be freer than any of his prophets or propagandists – to whom, according to tradition, he has revealed himself directly. Finally, human beings currently alive on Earth would be freer than those souls blessed with eternal life in heaven, for the latter – as stated in Paul's First Epistle to the Corinthians – see God 'face to face', or have what the theologians delightfully call a 'beatific vision' of him. Now, the idea that ordinary human beings should be freer than God himself, or freer than Abraham, Saint Paul or Muhammad, or even freer than souls blessed with eternal life, seems to me as theologically unacceptable as it is philosophically inconceivable.

The second reason that leads me to reject this explanation is that there is less freedom in ignorance than in knowledge. Such is the spirit of the Enlightenment, a spirit that is still alive today and still necessary if we wish to oppose obscurantism in all its forms. To claim that God conceals himself in order to protect our freedom is to posit that ignorance is one of the components of freedom. What teacher or parent worthy of the name could accept such an idea? If we are convinced that all children should attend school, it is because we think just the opposite; namely, that there is always greater freedom in knowledge than in ignorance. And we are right to think so. Such is the spirit of nondenominational education. Such, too, at least in part, is the spirit of the Gospels ('the truth shall make you free', as Saint John put it); such is spirit per se. Thus, it is unthinkable that God should keep us in the dark about his existence to preserve our freedom. Only knowledge, not ignorance, can set us free.

As for Kant's argument that if God were to reveal himself to us, all our actions would arise from hope and fear rather than duty, what it best proves is that the notions of reward and punishment, hope and fear, are intrinsically foreign to morality and, if absolutized, can only pervert it. With this we can agree. To act morally is indeed, as Kant has shown, to act independently of one's self-interest; this implies that we should do our duty 'without hoping to get anything out of it'. I agree with this statement, but it is more an argument against hell and heaven than it is a justification of human ignorance or divine concealment.

The third and final reason that leads me to reject this answer is that it seems to me incompatible with the idea of God as the Father, an idea that is both appealing and strongly established in our tradition. I have three children. When they were very young, their freedom consisted of obeying or disobeying, respecting or not respecting and doubtless also loving or not loving me. To do so, they had to be sure I existed! I had to look after them sufficiently for them to become free! What would you think of a father who hid from his children? 'I've never done anything to show them I exist,' he would tell you. 'They've never seen or met me; I wanted them to be free to believe in me or not, so I let them go on thinking they were orphans or illegitimate . . .' You'd think the man was ill, insane or a monster – and of course you would be right. What sort of Father would go on hiding as his children suffered through Auschwitz, the Gulag or Rwanda, as they were deported, humiliated, starved, tortured and murdered? The idea of a God who prefers to conceal himself is incompatible with the idea of God as Father. Indeed, it makes the very notion of God an oxymoron – any God who would do that would not be God.

'Weakness of the evidence? Speak for yourself!' some will say. 'I myself have a constant awareness that God is close by, listening to me and loving me.'

What can I answer, except that I have never felt anything of the sort? And it is not for lack of longing for such an experience and believing it possible. In my own life, however, faith never managed to replace presence. How empty of God I found the thronged churches! How strongly his silence reverberated behind our murmured prayers! Upon reaching adolescence, I admitted as much to my high-school chaplain: 'I keep praying and praying,' I told him, 'but God never answers me.' Being a man of great heart and spirit, the priest told me that 'God doesn't talk, because He is listening'. That set me dreaming for years. Eventually, however, I grew weary of his silence . . . and then suspicious. Did it mean that he was listening or that he didn't exist? How could I be certain? This is reminiscent of one of Woody Allen's one-liners: 'I'm devastated! I just learned my shrink has been dead for two years and I hadn't even noticed!' At least we can change shrinks. But what are we to do if there is only one God or if they all remain silent?

To each his own experience. One of the rare things I know for certain, in this area, is that God has never spoken to me. Actually, this is not so much an objection as it is a statement of fact. Other individuals, every bit as sincere as I am, seem to have experienced a presence, a love, a communication, an exchange . . . More power to them, if it helps them live. Humanity is far too weak and life far too difficult for people to go round spitting on each other's faiths. I loathe fanaticisms of all kinds, including atheistic fanaticism.

Still, evidence that is not shared by all and that other people can neither verify nor repeat remains fragile evidence indeed. How can we know what it is worth? Some people claim to have seen ghosts or communicated with the dead by turning tables. Should I believe them as well? I have no doubt that most of them are in good faith, but what does that prove? Hypocrisy may be exceptional; credulity, on the other hand, is not. In these areas, self-suggestion seems to me far more plausible than supernatural intervention.

Thus, weakness of the evidence. True, it proves nothing, but it is a powerful reason not to believe. If God doesn't show himself – at least, not to me and not to everyone – it might be because he feels like hiding. It might also be, and this seems to me a far simpler hypothesis, because he does not exist.

An Incomprehensible Explanation

My third argument, though not reducible to the first two, is, like them, a negative one. It involves explanations rather than proofs, rationality rather than evidence, conception rather than existence.

From a theoretical point of view, believing in God always amounts to trying to explain something we do not understand (the universe, life, human consciousness) by something we understand even less (God). How can such an attitude satisfy us intellectually?

This argument should not be misunderstood. Despite the spectacular progress made by science over the past three hundred years, we must never expect it to come up with anything like a proof of God's nonexistence. True, scientific progress often seems to bring about a regression in religion, at least temporarily. For all that, science can never come up with a global refutation of religion, much less replace it – because what explains the laws of nature? In our day and age, it would occur to no one to explain tides or eclipses by divine will. On the other hand, we are no more able today than yesterday to explain nature itself. This is why scientism, which might be described as the religion of science, is as open to doubt as all the other religions. It is also less poetic than the others – and more stupid, since it bypasses the very problem it purports to solve.

No, my argument is different. The point is not to replace religion with science, but to show that all the supernatural, nonscientific hypotheses advanced by religions to explain, for instance, the existence of the universe, life or human consciousness have one thing in common: they explain nothing because they hinge on the inexplicable! Thus, though definitely convenient, they are also useless. I'm well aware that I do not understand everything there is to understand about the universe, life and human consciousness. Much is unknown in these fields – this is what enables knowledge to progress. Much will always be unknown – this is what relegates us to mystery. But why would that mystery be God, especially given the fact that God can't be understood either, since ineffability is part of his definition? This is what makes his will, as Spinoza put it, 'a shelter for ignorance'. We take shelter in ignorance to explain what we do not understand. Religion becomes the universal solution, something like a theoretical master key – except that it opens only imaginary doors. What use is that? God explains everything, since he is all-powerful; but in vain, since he could just as well explain the opposite. The sun revolves around the earth? God wanted it that way. The earth revolves around the sun? God wanted it that way. This does not get us very far. And in either case, what is the explanation worth, given that God himself remains inexplicable and incomprehensible?

I would far rather accept mystery for what it is, namely the unknown and unknowable in which all knowledge and all existence are cloaked, the inexplicable that all explanations either presuppose or run up against. This is true from an ontological point of view. It is what I referred to earlier as the mystery of being. (Why is there something rather than nothing? We do not know, and we shall never know.) But it is also true from a physical or scientific point of view. Why are the laws of nature what they are? We don't know that, either, and since we can explain these laws only by other laws, it is unlikely that we shall ever know it. To call the mystery 'God' is not to dispel it; it is to opt for facile reassurance. Why is there God rather than nothing? Why do these laws exist rather than other laws? Faced with the silence of the universe, silence seems to me a far more appropriate response. Not only is it truer to the evidence and the mystery, but (as I shall try to show in the next chapter) it may also be more genuinely spiritual. Prayer and interpretation are no more or less than a way of slapping words on to the silence. Contemplation is preferable. Attention is preferable. Action is preferable. The world is far more interesting to me than the Bible or the Koran. It is far more mysterious than they are. It is vaster, since it contains them; more unfathomable; more astonishing; more stimulating, since we can transform it, whereas the holy books are reputed to be untouchable; and, last but not least, it is truer, because it is *entirely* true, something the Bible and the Koran, with all their inanities and inconsistencies, could never be, except in so far as they are part of the world (there is nothing inconsistent about a human text being inconsistent). Being is at once mysterious and self-evident. By contrast, what could be more banal, predictable and boring than the catechism? In this, it resembles us. 'God may have made us in His image,' as Voltaire put it, 'but we have paid him back in kind.' God is a shelter for ignorance and anthropomorphism. The universe, on the other hand, incites us to venture outward and take risks. It is the space of all knowledge and all action.

A friend of mine, a painter of no particular religious persuasion, once said to me, 'I'm not an atheist. I believe there is a mystery . . .' Ha! No kidding! I, too, believe there is a mystery! In fact, I believe there is not much else! True, many things can be explained – but not all things, not even the complete set of explicable things. As a result, all our explanations are shrouded in inexplicability. 'The truth is at the bottom of the abyss,' as Democritus put it, and the abyss is bottomless. This is our home. This is our destiny. Nothing could be more mysterious than the existence of the world, nature, being – yet we are within it (yes, at the very heart of being, the very heart of the mystery!). But this is exactly what is known as immanence, whereas God is described as being transcendent. The universe is mystery enough. Why invent another one?

Mystery belongs to no one. It is part of the human condition. It may even be part of being itself – if, as I believe, being can be explained only by itself, which is tantamount to saying that it is inexplicable. Far from being an objection against atheism, this innate and irreducible mystery of being is an objection against religion, or at least against a certain type of religiosity. This is what Hume meant when he asked, in his *Dialogues Concerning Natural Religion*, 'How do you Mystics, who maintain the absolute Incomprehensibility of the Deity, differ from Skeptics or Atheists, who assert, that the first Cause of All is unknown and unintelligible?' The objection is a more powerful one than it might seem at first sight. If the absolute is unknowable, what right do we have to believe that it is God?

Such are the limits of fideism. If faith surpasses all forms of reason, how can we know what we believe in? '*Credo quia absurdum*,' some believers say, along with Tertullian, Saint Augustine, Pascal or Kierkegaard – 'I believe because it is absurd.' More power to them! But why would the absurd be God? And how could it be a convincing argument?

Such, too, are the limits of deism, which is faith without revelation, church or doctrine. To be a deist is to believe in God without claiming to know him. It is a humble, minimal, abstract form of faith. But what does it believe in? 'I believe in God,' a reader once told me in a letter, 'but not the God of religions, for religions are merely human. The true God is unknowable . . .' Fine. But if we can't know him at all, how can we be sure he is God?

Such, lastly, are the limits of the negative or 'apophatic'

theologies (from the Greek *apophasis*, negation). We can conceive of God only by analogy. By analogy with what? With the believer. This is the meaning of the often-quoted passage from Montesquieu's *Persian Letters*: 'Were triangles to invent a God, they would give him three sides.' It is hardly surprising that humanity's gods should be anthropomorphic. This was true of the various Greek and Roman gods, and it is true, though differently, of the 'one God' of the three monotheisms. Of necessity, he is conceived by analogy, either with what we are or with what we know: God is to nature as the artist and artisan are to the objects they produce (the architect to the house, the clockmaker to the clock, and so forth); he is to humanity as a father to his children or as a sovereign to his subjects; he is to the Church as a husband to his wife . . . Given this, anything and everything we can say positively about God will bear the mark of anthropomorphism. The religions of the Book are no exception. Judaism and Islam prohibited images of God, but this did not suffice to abolish the imagination! Anthropomorphism runs more deeply than that; it affects the very concept of divinity. Such is the cost of analogy. To conceive of God as a spiritual, personal creator is already to indulge in anthropomorphism, and yet these traits are part of his very definition. To refer to him as a father is also to indulge in anthropomorphism, and yet this is how the Gospels and the Church describe him; one need only re-read the Lord's Prayer and the Credo. To characterize him as just, powerful and wise, as the Bible and the Koran do, is once again to indulge in anthropomorphism; the same is true of his loving, compassionate or merciful nature . . . But what could possibly be said about God, above and beyond anthropomorphism, if not precisely *nothing*? This sends us back to the first hypothesis of Plato's *Parmenides*: If Oneness exists, nothing can be said about it. 'There is not even a name for it; it can be neither defined nor known, neither felt nor judged.' But if this is the case, there is no reason – and, indeed, no *way* – to think of it as a God. Where the absolute is concerned, all forms of anthropomorphism are naïve or ridiculous. Faced with the ineffable, it is best to remain silent.

This is where the negative theologies come in. They do not venture to say what God is (since that is impossible), only what he is not. He is not a body, he does not exist in space or time, he is neither a monarch nor an artist, neither a created thing nor an old man with a long white beard . . . Fine. To quote an old Jewish joke, he is not a long garden hose, either – nor is he a comprehensive insurance plan, a gifted and benevolent psychotherapist, a pet, a husband, a lover (Canticle of Canticles notwithstanding), a super-cop, a computer, a software program, or a winning combination in roulette. I readily agree with all of this, but what, in the final analysis, does it teach us about what he is? 'We affirm nothing and deny nothing,' declared the thinker commonly referred to as Dionysius the Areopagite, 'for the single and perfect Cause is beyond any affirmation, and its transcendence is beyond any negation.' This would seem to reduce us to a choice between silence and ecstasy, which is singularly convenient for believers. How can silence be refuted? How can ecstasy be discussed? Thus the very concept of God becomes empty or inconceivable: though the word has a meaning (a *signified*, as linguists would call it), no one can adequately think through what it is intended to designate (its *referent*, if it has one). This may not prove that God does not exist (how could anyone prove the nonexistence of something in which they don't believe?), it does make the position of those who believe in him exceedingly fragile. If God is inconceivable, then nothing justifies our conceiving of him as a Subject, a Person, a Creator, a Protector, a Benefactor, the embodiment of Justice or Love. This, as Hume recognized, is where mysticism can agree with atheism. If nothing can be said of God, then neither can it be said that he exists or that he is God. All the names of God are either human or anthropomorphic, yet a God without a name would no longer be God. Ineffability is not an argument. Silence is not a religion.

It might be objected that even atheism cannot escape the alternative between anthropomorphism and ineffability. 'If all discourse on God is anthropomorphic,' a Catholic priest once told me, 'then it applies to those who deny his existence as much as to those who affirm it.' Not quite, it seems to me. To believe in God is to ratify, at least partially, the anthropomorphism that is inevitably implied by the notion of God. It is to think either that the absolute resembles us (that it is a Subject, a Person, a Spirit . . .) or that we resemble it (that we were made 'in its image'). To be an atheist, on the other hand, is to think that, while the idea of God may well resemble us (which is only natural, given that we invented it), ultimate or basic reality does *not* resemble us; there is nothing human, personal or spiritual about it. That is an important difference indeed! Believers and atheists may (or rather, must) use the same concept of God, but the former at least partially accept the concept's anthropomorphism (yes, they say, God truly is a Subject or a Spirit; yes, he truly did make us in his image), whereas the latter deny it (the ultimate reality is neither a subject nor a spirit; rather, it is matter, energy, nature 'without subject and without end'). Religion and irreligion both use the same concept, and both are without proof, but that is no reason to conflate them!

In a word, where God is concerned, there is no way to escape from the alternative between silence (God as inconceivable, ineffable, incomprehensible) and anthropomorphism (a God too human and too comprehensible to be God). This is clearly a liability for religion: silence says not enough (why would the unspeakable be God?), whereas anthropomorphism says too much (why would the absolute be human?).

Excess of Evil

This brings me to the three positive arguments that incite me not only to not believe in God (the position of negative atheism, virtually indistinguishable from agnosticism) but to believe that God does not exist (the position of positive atheism, that is, atheism in the strict sense of the word).

The first of these arguments is at once the oldest, the most banal and the most powerful: it is the existence of evil, or rather its amplitude, its atrocity, its outrageousness. Is this in fact a positive argument? Definitely, in so far as evil is a *fact* that not only points up a weakness of religion (as was already the case for the three preceding arguments) but also provides a strong reason to be an atheist. This argument seems so self-evident and has been made so many times since Epicurus and Lucretius that one almost hesitates to return to it. Yet return to it we must, for evil and religions continue to exist.

Epicurus, as was his wont, went straight to the heart of the issue – which heart, according to Lactantius, he summarized in four hypotheses. Since none of them is plausible (this is what I sometimes refer to as the *tetralemma* of religion), the hypothesis of a creator God is not plausible either.

Either God wanted to eliminate evil and could not; or he could and did not want to; or he neither could nor wanted to; or he could and wanted to. If he wanted to and could not, he is impotent, which cannot be the case for God; if he could and did not want to, he is evil, which is foreign to God's nature. If he neither could nor wanted to, he is both

impotent and evil, in which case he is not God. If he
both wanted to and could – the only hypothesis that
corresponds to God – where does evil come from, or
why did God not eliminate it?

Since the fourth hypothesis – the only one in conformity with our notion of God – is refuted by reality itself (the
existence of evil), it must be concluded that no God created
the world or governs it, either because there is no God or
because (as Epicurus believed) the gods are concerned neither with us nor with the order and disorder of the
universe, which they did not create and which they in no
way govern. Thus there is no such thing as either providence or destiny: we have nothing to expect from the gods,
and nothing to fear from them either. Indeed, Lucretius
added, its very imperfection shows us 'that in no wise the
nature of all things/For us was fashioned by a power
divine'. On this theme, the poet wrote some of his most
tragically beautiful verses: life is too difficult, humanity too
weak, labour too exhausting, pleasures too frivolous or rare,
pain too frequent or atrocious, chance too unfair and hap-
hazard for us to be able to believe that so imperfect a world
is of divine origin!

This is what is traditionally known as the problem of
evil, but it is a problem only for believers. For atheists, evil
is a fact, one that needs to be acknowledged, confronted
and surmounted, if possible, but one that is in no way difficult to comprehend. The world was made neither for us

nor by us. Why would it correspond in every way to our desires, needs and demands? 'The world is not a nursery', as Freud put it. And Alain: 'The Earth made us no promises'. For an atheist, the existence of evil goes without saying. It is less of a theoretical problem than a practical obstacle and an incontrovertible fact.

For a believer, on the other hand, it is impossible to justify the ubiquity of evil in a world created by an infinitely kind and almighty God. It is a case of fact becoming an objection or a mystery. Leibniz summed it up in two questions in his *Theodicy*: 'If God exists, whence evil? If he does not exist, whence good?' This distributes the burden of proof too equally. Despite their apparent symmetry, the two questions do not have the same weight. The existence of good (in the form of pleasure, compassion and love) can be adequately explained by nature and history. But how can the existence of evil – an evil so widespread, atrocious and unjust – be compatible with the existence, omnipotence and infinite perfection of God?

Let us now enter into a bit of detail. That the world should contain evil might be comprehensible and acceptable, even from the point of view of believers, as the price we must pay for Creation. If the world contained no evil, it would be perfect, but if it were perfect, it would be God and there would be no world. Such was Simone Weil's reasoning when she expounded upon the Pauline theme of exinanition or *kenosis* (renunciation) – and perhaps even, without knowing it, the ancient theme of mystical Judaism known as *tsimtsum*. Out of love, God emptied himself of his divinity and withdrew, in order that – by virtue of this withdrawal (creation), this distance (space), this expectancy (time), this lack of God (the universe) – something other than himself could exist. Creating, for God, did not mean adding more goodness to the infinite goodness he already was (how could God do better than God, since he was all possible goodness?); it meant consenting to be not all. Thus the creation of the world was not, as human beings naïvely believe, an increase or a progression; rather, it was a subtraction, a diminishing – something like an amputation of God by himself. 'Creation', Weil wrote, 'is for God an act not of expansion but of withdrawal, of renunciation. God and all His creatures are less than God alone. God accepted this limitation. He emptied himself of a part of being. Already, in the act of his divinity, he had emptied himself – which is why Saint John says the Lamb was slaughtered as of the creation of the world.' What could be more natural than the fact that the world contains evil, given that the world can only exist on condition that it not be God?

Fine. This might suffice to explain the presence of evil in the world . . . but did there have to be so *much* of it? Despite the great admiration and tenderness I feel for Simone Weil, this is what I've always found it impossible to conceive and accept.

In these matters, experience is more eloquent than metaphysics, and sensitivity may be more important than experience. Still, even for optimists like Leibniz, the existence of evil is incontrovertible. Is the same true of the existence of good? If you like. But nature suffices to explain both, whereas the existence of God would make both incomprehensible – the first by excess, the second by insufficiency. There is too much horror in the world, too much suffering, too much injustice – and too little happiness – for the concept of its creation by an almighty, infinitely kind God to be tenable in my eyes.

True, human beings are often responsible for suffering and injustice. But who created humanity? Believers will answer that God created us free, which freedom includes our ability to do evil . . . This merely sends us back to the dilemma mentioned above: does this imply, then, that we are freer than God, who, being perfect, is capable of doing only good? And even leaving this difficulty aside, why would God have made us so weak, cowardly, violent, avid, pretentious and overbearing? Why are there so many nasty or mediocre human beings, so few heroes and saints? Why is there so much egotism, so much envy and hatred and so little generosity and love? Banality of evil; rarity of good! It seems to me that a God, even while allowing us freedom and imperfection, would have come up with a better ratio.

Finally, and perhaps most important, there is the suffering that has been going on for thousands of years and for which humanity is *not* responsible. The children who have died of illnesses, often after enduring terrible pain. The millions of women who have died (and still do die, in some parts of the world) in childbirth, torn apart body and soul. The mothers of these children, and (if they are still alive) the mothers of these mothers, who, unable to give them relief or assistance, could only sit there looking on helplessly as the horror unfolded. Who will dare throw original sin in their faces? The countless deaths caused by cancer (not all of which can be chalked up to the environment or modern lifestyle), by the plague, malaria, cholera, Alzheimer's disease, autism, schizophrenia, mucoviscidosis, myopathy, multiple sclerosis, Charcot's disease, Huntington's chorea . . . The deaths caused by earthquakes, tidal waves, hurricanes, droughts, floods and volcanic eruptions . . . It could only be laughable or obscene to explain away the misery of the just and the suffering of children by original sin. 'We must be born guilty,' wrote Pascal, 'or God would be unjust.' There is a third, far simpler possibility: namely, that God does not exist.

Animals suffered long before the appearance of human beings. Billions of animals, belonging to millions of species, survived by devouring billions of other animals, their only offence being that they were too weak or too slow to escape their clutches. I am not a member of the RSPCA, but one need only watch a few animal films on television: hour after hour, one sees tigers dismembering gazelles; big fish devouring little fish; birds gobbling down earthworms; insects munching on other insects . . . I don't hold it against them; they are only doing their jobs as living creatures, but how can the endless suffering of their prey be fitted into a divine plan? Modern ecologists protest against force-feeding geese, and perhaps they are justified in doing so, but that's nothing compared with the invention of carnivores! Life, such as God is believed to have created it, and long before the appearance of *Homo sapiens*, is horrifyingly violent and unjust. It is like an unending massacre. From this point of view, Buddha's first 'holy truth' – namely, that 'all life is suffering', *sarvam dukkham* – unfortunately seems much closer to what we experience than the teachings of the three monotheisms! Pain is incalculable. Misery is incalculable. I'm not denying that pleasures and joys also exist. I'm simply repeating that nature suffices to explain them, whereas the hypothesis of God makes horror inexplicable.

Faced with the enormity and irrefutability of evil, some believers choose to reverse the usual line of argument, invoking not God's omnipotence but his impotence or weakness. This is a variant of *kenosis* or *tsimtsum*. Hans Jonas, for instance, in *The Concept of God After Auschwitz*, insists that we need to take recent history into account in all its renewed horror, excess and atrocity. The Holocaust makes the very notion of an all-powerful God intolerable. Thus, we must renounce that notion from now on and accept, on the contrary, the tragic weakness of a God in process, a suffering God, a God who, as Jonas puts it (in a phrase reminiscent of Simone Weil, though he doesn't quote her), has 'divested himself of his divinity' – a disarmed God, who had to renounce his might in order to create the world and humankind . . . Well, why not? In the face of horror, this is certainly preferable to Leibniz's shocking rationalizations. It does not, however, diminish the horror.

The theme of a feeble God, advanced by Dietrich Bonhoeffer during the Second World War and expounded upon by several Christian theologians of today, is said to be justified by the figure of Christ himself. The life of Jesus began and ended in weakness; its symbols are the manger and the cross, the vulnerable baby born between ox and donkey and the innocent man crucified between two thieves. Alain, who was Weil's mentor, wrote some striking pages on this theme. In *The Gods*, he, too, suggested that 'power withdrew'. And his *Preliminaries to Mythology* contain the following paragraph, which I have never been able to read without great emotion:

If anyone dares to go on talking to me about an almighty God, I answer: that was a pagan god, and now we have gone beyond him. The new god is weak, crucified, humiliated; such is his state; such is his essence. Do not hedge on this; meditate upon the image. Do not say that the spirit will win out, that in the end it will have the power and the glory, the guards and the prisons, and the crown of gold. No. The images speak too loudly; they cannot be falsified. What the spirit will have is the crown of thorns.

In Alain's view, however, this god was all the weaker
for not being God. He was merely the spirit ('forever
humiliated, scorned, crucified, forever rising from the dead
on the third day'); indeed he existed only in so far as he
became human. This is true humanism; it is true spirituality, but without a Church, without a dogma, without a
God. I find it more difficult to accept the weak God as
others construe him: powerful enough to create the universe and mankind, and possibly enough to bring us back
from the dead, but not enough to save the life of a child, or
the lives of his people.

Other believers take refuge in their very inability to
solve the problem. Evil, they say, is 'a mystery'. I don't
believe it is. Rather, I see evil as one of the few certainties
there is. As Pascal remarked with his usual lucidity, 'We are
well acquainted with evil and falsehood,' but not with good
and truth. What is mysterious, or at least what makes evil
mysterious, is their God. That mystery being an imaginary
one, I would just as soon dispense with it. Far better to recognize evil for what it is, in all its banality and excess, its
atrocious, admissible self-evidence; far better to confront it
and combat it while we can. This is no longer religion but
mortality; it is no longer faith but action.

Human Mediocrity

My fifth argument, also in favour of atheism has to do less
with the world than with human beings: the more I get to

know them, the less I can believe in God. Let's say I don't have a sufficiently lofty conception of humanity in general or myself in particular to believe that a God could be at the origin of this species and this individual. Everywhere I look, there is too much mediocrity, too much pettiness, too much of what Montaigne called nothingness or vanity – 'of all the vanities, the vainest is man'. What a poor result for omnipotence! Some will object that God may have done better elsewhere. Well, perhaps he has. Is that any reason to be satisfied with such a lousy job here? What would you think of an artist who, on the pretext that he has produced masterpieces for other people, would saddle you with his trash? You might say this often happens with today's artists; still, it is hardly acceptable for One who is supposed to be all-powerful and infinitely kind. In brief, that God should have agreed to turn out a work as mediocre as humankind seems to me, to put it mildly, highly implausible.

'God created man in his own image,' we read in Genesis. This should cast doubt on the original. The idea of man descending from the monkey seems to me far more credible, far more suggestive – and far *truer to life*. Darwin is a merciful master indeed.

Does this mean that misanthropes are right? Definitely not! Man is not basically evil. He may be basically mediocre, but that's not his fault. He does what he can with what he has or what he is, but what he is is not much and there is not much he can do. This should make us indulgent towards him – and even, occasionally, admiring of him. Materialism, as Julien La Mettrie put it, is the antidote for misanthropy: *because* men are animals, it is pointless to hate or even despise them. Were we copies of God, we would be either ridiculous or terrifying. For animals produced by nature, we are not without our qualities and merits. Not bad, given our base beginnings! Who, a hundred thousand years ago, would have believed that these large monkeys would some day walk on the moon, produce Michelangelo and Mozart, Shakespeare and Einstein, invent the notion of human and even animal rights? We do our best, for instance, to protect endangered species such as whales and elephants – and rightly so. But were humanity itself to become an endangered species, as it might one day, whales and elephants would not lift a fin or a trunk to save us. Ecology is proper to humankind (yes, despite pollution, or rather because of it), and even animal rights can exist only for human beings. That says a lot about our species.

A religion of man? Definitely not. What a sorry god man would make! Humanism is not a religion; it is an ethics (which includes our responsibilities towards other animal species). Man is not our God; he is our neighbour. Humanity is not our church; it is our demand. To quote Montaigne's phrase again, our task is that of 'playing the man properly', and it is an unending one. Ours is an illusionless humanism that cares about protecting our species, especially from itself. We must forgive humanity, and ourselves, for being what we are – neither angels nor beasts, as

Montaigne put it before Pascal; neither slaves nor super-men: 'They want to break away from themselves and escape from the man. That is madness: instead of turning into angels, they turn into beasts; instead of raising them-selves, they lower themselves. These transcendental humours frighten me, like lofty and inaccessible places.' Lucidity suffices, and is worth far more.

Man is finite; man is exceptional. Grotesque if taken as an imitation of God, *Homo sapiens* is by far the most extra-ordinary of animals. Human beings have astonishingly complex and flexible brains; they are capable of love, revolt and creativity; they have invented science and art, morals and law, religion and irreligion, philosophy and humour, gastronomy and eroticism . . . Not bad, for an animal! No other animal species could have achieved humanity's best – or its worst. This should suffice to prove our singularity. But to jump to the conclusion that we were created by God . . . *What?* Our pettiness, our narcissism and egotism, our rivalries, hatreds, resentments and jealousies, our distrac-tions and satisfactions of personal comfort or self-love, our nasty or ignominious deeds . . . Do they really need a God to explain them? Poor God! If he exists, he certainly must be bored . . . or ashamed! Spend a single day surfing chan-nels on television, and then – in the face of so much stupidity, violence and vulgarity – ask yourself the simple question, How can an omnipotent, omniscient Being have wished for *this*? It might be objected that God is not responsible for our TV programmes, and this is true. But he is credited with having made humanity, and humanity is responsible for TV ratings and programmes. Faced with the flagrant mediocrity of our species, how can we believe it was made by an infinitely perfect Creator?

Am I exaggerating? I don't think so. Of necessity, I am simplifying, taking shortcuts. For instance, I have chosen to examine one side of the question more than the other. I am well aware that masterpieces, genius and heroism exist (sometimes even on TV!). I also know that the inoffensive by far outnumber the true villains. With respect to the subject at hand, however, the two sides of humanity (light and darkness, greatness and pettiness) have neither the same relevance nor the same force. It is far easier to reconcile man's grandeur with a natural origin than it is to reconcile his 'miserable nature', as Pascal called it, with a divine origin! Natural selection suffices to explain our capacity for love and courage, intelligence and compassion. All of these things are selective advantages that make the transmission of our genes more probable. That we are capable of such hatred, violence and pettiness, on the other hand, seems to me beyond the explanatory reach of any theology, whereas Darwinism can explain it with no problem. Need I add that I myself am no exception to this rule? The better I know myself, the more difficult I find it to believe our origin is divine. The better I know others, too. Believing in God, I once wrote, is a sin of pride. It is imagining a grand cause for a meagre effect. Atheism, conversely, is a form of humil-

ity. No doubt about it: we are children of the earth –
humus, whence 'humility'. We would do better to accept
our earthly nature and invent the sky that goes along
with it.

Desire and Illusion

The sixth and final argument that incites me to come down
in favour of atheism is perhaps the most subjective one –
but, of course, were we not subjects, the question itself
would not exist.

What is at stake in this argument? Nothing less than *us*
– and our wish for God. Yes, I desperately wish that God
existed, and I see this as a particularly convincing reason
not to believe he does. This is only apparently contradictory. To be an atheist is not necessarily to be against God.
Why would I be against what does not exist? Personally, I
would go even further and admit that I would definitely
prefer that there be a God. This is just why, in my eyes, all
religions are suspicious.

'Philosophy makes no bones about it,' wrote Marx as a
young man (in his 1841 dissertation on Democritus and
Epicurus). 'It adopts Prometheus's profession of faith: "I
hate all the gods."' This is youthful naïveté. No, philosophy
per se does not hate the gods, nor, indeed, do all philosophers; the greatest among them, including the atheists, refer
to them with respect. And concerning the Christian God in
particular (the only one I have frequented personally, at

least in my imagination), I see no reason to hate him. Quite the opposite, in fact – what could be more likeable than a God of love? Who would not dream of having one? But this is no reason to believe in him, for what do dreams prove? We are in favour of justice, too, but that hardly proves it exists. As Alain rightly put it, 'Justice does not exist, which is why we need to create it.' Yes, we must create it as best we can, and it turns out that we *can*, to some extent. Wanting is important. Indeed, wanting is sufficient, provided that justice is more than a pose or a discourse. But who could create God? It is impossible. If he existed, he might be responsible for us – but if he does not, we can hardly be responsible for him.

God is the absolute dream, the dream of the absolute – an infinity of love, justice and truth. I am all for it, just as most people are, by which I mean that I would definitely prefer for such a thing to exist, but this is no reason to believe that it does. Indeed, it is a strong reason not to. Some people are surprised to hear this: 'If you would prefer God to exist,' they say, 'then you should believe in him!' No, just the opposite! Just *because* I would prefer God to exist, I have excellent reasons to doubt his existence. I would also prefer war, poverty, injustice and hatred to disappear completely. But if someone came up to me tomorrow and told me they had, I would say he was a dreamer, a victim of wishful thinking – or else, if he tried to force his dream on me, a terrorist.

Why would I prefer God to exist? Because he would

fulfil my deepest longings. This in itself would be enough to dissuade me, were I tempted to believe: there would be every reason to fear that a belief so strikingly congruent with our longings was invented to fulfil them, if only in the imagination. The least we can say is that reality, as a general rule, does not entirely live up to our expectations.

What do we wish for more than anything else? Leaving aside our base or vulgar desires, which have no need of God to be fulfilled, what we wish for most is: first, not to die, at least not completely, not irreversibly; second, to be reunited with the loved ones we have lost; third, for justice and peace to triumph; finally and perhaps most importantly, to be loved.

Now, what does religion tell us – and the Christian religion in particular? That we shall not die, or not really; that we shall rise from the dead and thus be reunited with the loved ones we have lost; that justice and peace will prevail in the end; and, finally, that we are already the object of an infinite love. Who could ask for more? No one, of course! This is what makes religion so very suspicious: as the saying goes, it is too good to be true! Such was Freud's argument, in *The Future of an Illusion*: 'Of course it would be very nice if there were a God who had created the world and a Providence filled with goodness, a moral order of the universe and life after death, and yet it is very strange that all of this is exactly what we might wish for ourselves.' Such was already Nietzsche's argument, in *The Antichrist*: 'Faith saves, therefore it lies.' God is too desirable to be true; religion is too reassuring to be credible.

What Freud and Nietzsche are engaged in here, and what I'm attempting to engage in with them, is in effect the reversal (though from another standpoint) of the ontological proof: just *because* God is defined as supremely perfect ('a being', we might say along with Anselm, 'such that no better one could be wished for'), it is advisable not to believe in him.

It might also be seen as a reversal of 'Pascal's wager'. Being more lucid in this respect than Descartes or Leibniz, Pascal was convinced that there neither was nor could be a proof of God's existence – and that if there indeed was one, what it would prove would not be God, because only truths can be proven, but 'truth without charity is not God'. A provable God would be 'the God of philosophers and scholars', not that of Jesus Christ. However, Pascal added, though we cannot *prove* God, we must *bet* on his existence. Why? By virtue of the calculation of probabilities or game theory – a discipline that Pascal, along with Fermat, contributed to inventing. In religion, as Pascal explained in a now-famous fragment of his *Thoughts*, we have everything to win and nothing to lose. Mathematics can calculate this quite accurately. What is a good bet? One in which the ratio between the outlay and the possible gain is proportionate to the probability of the latter. If we play heads or tails, for instance, the probability of winning being one out of two, the hoped-for winnings need to be at least double the initial outlay for the game to be worth it. If it is lower, we should refuse to bet; if higher, it is in our interest to accept it. Now, where God is concerned, or rather our belief in God, the possible gain ('an infinity of infinitely happy life', as Pascal puts it) is infinitely greater than the outlay (our miserable, mortal earthly existence). Thus, given the not-nil probability of winning, the not-infinite probability of losing (the existence of God is possible), and the infinite disparity between the outlay and the winnings, we should not hesitate to bet that God exists. Pascal summed it up in a sentence that has been quoted countless times: 'If you win, you win all; if you lose, you lose nothing.'

The argument, while it may be mathematically impeccable, seems to me theologically dubious. Why should grace depend on the calculation of probabilities? How could my salvation possibly hinge on a bet? God is not a croupier. Nothing prevents me from betting on his existence and choosing to be damned, or betting on his nonexistence and choosing to be saved. But even leaving aside the theological objection, Pascal's wager seems to me particularly unacceptable from a philosophical point of view. Reflection is not a game of chance. Conscience is not a casino. Why should we subject our reason to our self-interest, our minds to the calculation of profits and losses, our life philosophy to a winning combination? That would be unworthy of us, and of reason, and of Pascal. His wager was invented not for himself – for he derived his faith from

God alone – but for libertines, who wished to believe only in their own pleasure. Here is where hedonism and utilitarianism meet their limits. I am not a gambler, I am a thinking spirit. What I care about most is not my own advantage but truth – and nothing can guarantee that the two go hand in hand. Indeed, it is rather unlikely that they should, given the particular nature of my advantage and the universal nature of truth. Thus, given that I have neither proof nor experience of the existence of God, the very advantage I might have in believing in him (as Pascal's wager shows) should make me wary of the temptation to do so, or be a powerful reason not to. Reality is so rarely congruent with our desires – why would it make an exception on such an important issue?

All religions are optimistic. Even Manichaeanism announced the ultimate triumph of Good. This says a lot about religions.

Gospel, in Greek, means 'good news'. This says a lot about Christianity. Such is the spirit of the Beatitudes; no wonder we find them so moving and gratifying. The kingdom for the poor; comfort for the afflicted; the ultimate triumph of life over death and peace over war; an eternity of infinite happiness (at least for the just) – who could ask for more? But this is exactly what makes it improbable. Given an alleged reality that nothing attests but which corresponds to our most powerful wishes, we have every reason to suspect it of being the expression of those very wishes, and indeed (as Freud says) directly derived from them – to suspect it, in other words, of having the structure of an illusion.

What is an illusion? It is not, as Freud pointed out, the same thing as an error; and, indeed, illusions are not necessarily false. An illusion is 'a belief derived from human wishes' – a desiring credo, you might call it, or a credulous desire. This is corroborated by the everyday meaning of the term: to be in the thrall of an illusion is to indulge in wishful thinking. Take, for instance, a poor young girl who believes that she will some day marry a prince or a millionaire. It may be highly unlikely that her dream will come true, but, as Freud notes, it is not impossible. The young girl may turn out to be right. Nevertheless, she is in the thrall of an illusion, for the simple reason that her belief is founded not in knowledge but in her own desire. Thus, illusion is not a particular sort of error; it is a particular sort of belief. To be deluded is to believe that something is true because one wants it to be true. Humanly speaking, nothing could be more comprehensible. Philosophically speaking, nothing could be more dubious.

This sixth argument, if juxtaposed with the third (the 'incomprehensible explanation'), forms a sort of chiasmus that reinforces both: God is too incomprehensible, from a metaphysical point of view, not to be dubious (if you don't understand something, how can you know whether it is God or a chimera?); religion is too comprehensible, from an anthropological point of view, not to be suspicious.

Let's say I want to purchase an apartment in the United

States – in one of Manhattan's most elegant neighbour-hoods, for instance, with a stunning view of Central Park. I would like the place to have at least six bedrooms, two bathrooms, a balcony facing south, and of course it must be in tip-top shape and cost no more than a hundred thou-sand dollars. 'I haven't found it yet,' I might tell you, 'but I'm still looking. I feel confident – I believe in it!' You would say I was deluding myself, and of course you would be right. That by no means proves I am wrong. I could run into an insane real-estate agent or an unusually generous patron of the arts. It does, however, make my position very tenuous. Deep down, all of you are convinced that my search will be fruitless. And now, if I tell you I believe in a God who is immortal, omniscient, all-powerful, perfectly kind and just, loving and merciful, you find that more plau-sible than a stunning six-bedroom apartment on the Upper East Side of Manhattan for less than a hundred thousand dollars? Then you have either a paltry notion of God or an exalted notion of real estate.

'We are inclined by nature to find it easy to believe what we hope for, and hard to believe what we fear,' Spinoza wrote in his *Ethics*. 'Whence,' he added, 'the superstitions by which men are everywhere dominated.' All the more reason to be wary of our beliefs when they start resembling our hopes too closely! Who doesn't hope for the ultimate triumph of peace and justice? Who doesn't want to be loved? Who wouldn't long for the definitive victory of life over death? If it was up to me, God would have started existing long ago! Since it is clearly *not* up to me, however, I have no choice but to admit that our very longing for God, which is the longing of all small children to be loved and protected by what Freud called a 'transfigured Father', is one of the most powerful arguments against the belief in his existence.

The Right to Not Believe

A final word to sum up and conclude this chapter: we have discussed six major arguments, the first three of which lead me not to believe in God and the latter three of which lead me to believe that he does not exist. They are:

1. The weakness of the opposing arguments, the so-called proofs of God's existence.
2. Common experience: if God existed, he should be easier to see or sense.
3. My refusal to explain something I cannot understand by something I understand even less.
4. The enormity of evil.
5. The mediocrity of mankind.
6. Last but not least, the fact that God corresponds so perfectly to our wishes that there is every reason to think he was invented to fulfil them, at least in fantasy; this makes religion an illusion in the Freudian sense of the term.

Taken separately or together, these arguments by no means constitute a proof of God's nonexistence. I said as much at the outset. Does God exist? We do not know. We never shall know – not in this life, at least. Whence the question of whether to believe in him or not. The reader now knows why, for my part, I do not: first, because no argument proves his existence; second, because no experience attests it; and lastly because, to my mind, it is more appropriate to respond to being with mystery, to evil with horror and compassion, to mediocrity with mercy and humour (had God created us in his image and absolutely free, we would be unforgivable) and, finally, to our wishes and illusions with lucidity. Such are my reasons, or at least the ones among them that I find the most convincing. Far be it from me to force them on anyone else. I insist only on having the right to express them publicly and submit them to others for discussion, as is only natural.

What is fanaticism? Fanaticism is mistaking one's faith for knowledge or attempting to impose it through force. The two almost invariably go hand in hand: dogmatism and terrorism are mutually reinforcing. This is a double offence – against intelligence and against freedom. Thus we must combat it doubly – through lucidity and democracy. Freedom of conscience is a human right and a prerequisite of intelligence.

Religion is a right, and so is irreligion. Thus, both must be protected – if necessary, one against the other – and protecting them means ensuring that they are not imposed through force. This is why the separation of church and state is the most precious heritage of the Enlightenment. Today's world is rediscovering how very fragile that heritage is. All the more reason to defend it against all forms of fundamentalism and pass it on to our children.

Freedom of thought is the only good that is perhaps more precious than peace, for the simple reason that, without it, peace would merely be another name for servitude.

Chapter III

Can There Be an Atheist Spirituality?

L et us conclude with what, to my mind, is most important of all – not God, not religion, not atheism, but spiritual life. Some will express surprise: 'What? You, an atheist, take an interest in spiritual life?' Of course I do. Not believing in God does not prevent me from having a spirit, nor does it exempt me from having to use it.

People can do without religion, as I showed in the first chapter, but they cannot do without communion, fidelity and love. Nor can they do without spirituality. Why should they? Being an atheist by no means implies that I should castrate my soul! The human spirit is far too important a matter to be left up to priests, mullahs or spiritualists. It is our noblest part, or, rather, our highest function, the thing that makes us not only different from other animals (for we are animals as well), but greater than and superior to them. 'Man is a metaphysical animal,' said Schopenhauer – and therefore, I would add, a spiritual animal as well. This is our way of inhabiting the universe and the absolute, which inhabit us. What could be better, loftier or more fascinating than the spirit? Not believing in God is no reason to amputate a part of our humanity, especially not *that* part!

Renouncing religion by no means implies renouncing spiritual life.

Can There Be a Godless Spirituality?

Spirituality is the life of the spirit. But what is the spirit? 'A thing that thinks,' said Descartes, 'that is to say, that doubts, affirms, denies, that knows a few things, that is ignorant of many, that wills, that desires, that also imagines and perceives.' And I would add: a thing that loves, that does not love, that contemplates, that remembers, that mocks or jokes . . . Little does it matter whether the thing in question is the brain, as I believe it to be, or an immaterial substance, as was Descartes's conviction. Whatever it is, we use it to think, to want and to imagine. What is the spirit? It is the power to think, in so far as it gives us access to truth, universality or laughter. It is likely that without the brain, this ability would be able to do nothing at all or would not even exist. On the other hand, without this ability, the brain would be an organ like any other.

The spirit is not a substance. Rather, it is a function, a capacity, an act (the act of thinking, willing, imagining, making wisecracks . . .) – and this act, at least, is irrefutable, since nothing can be refuted without it. 'The spirit is not a hypothesis,' as Alain put it, because hypotheses can exist only by and through the spirit.

But let us move away from metaphysics. In spiritual matters, the real problem is the extension of the word *spirit*.

Taken in its broadest sense, spirituality can be said to include virtually all aspects of human life and *spiritual* is more or less synonymous with 'mental' or 'psychic'. Today, this sense of the word has pretty much gone out of use, and when people talk about spirituality they are usually referring to a rather limited part of our inner life (though it may contemplate limitlessness) – the part that involves the absolute, the infinite and the eternal. It is, in a sense, the spirit's furthermost point and its greatest amplitude.

As shown in the first chapter, we are finite beings who open on to infinity. It can now be added: we are ephemeral beings who open on to eternity, and relative beings who open on to the absolute. This 'openness' is the spirit itself. Metaphysics means thinking about these things; spirituality means experiencing them, exercising them, living them.

This is what distinguishes spirituality from religion, which is merely one of its possible forms. The two can be conflated only by virtue of metonymy or misnomer. They are as whole and part, genus and species. All religions involve spirituality, at least to some extent, but all forms of spirituality are not religious. Whether or not you believe in God, the supernatural or the sacred, you are confronted with the infinite, the eternal and the absolute – and with yourself. Nature suffices. The truth suffices. Our own transitory finiteness suffices. Otherwise we could not conceive of ourselves as being relative, ephemeral or finite.

To be an atheist is not to deny the existence of the absolute; rather, it is to deny its transcendence, its spirituality, its personality. It is to deny that the absolute is God. But to be not-God is not to not be! Otherwise we ourselves, and the world itself, would not be! If the word *absolute* is taken in its most ordinary sense, as that which exists independently of any condition, relationship or point of view – for instance, the sum of all conditions (nature), all relationships (the universe) and all possible or actual points of view (the truth) – its existence is impossible to refute. The sum of all conditions is necessarily unconditional, the sum of all relations is necessarily absolute, and the sum of all points of view can hardly be a single one.

This is what is known as naturalism, immanentism or materialism. These three metaphysical outlooks, though not always identical, tend to converge, at least concerning the subject at hand and also, at least negatively, in their essentials: they reject the idea of the supernatural, the idea of transcendence and the idea of an immaterial spirit – and thus of a creator God. I endorse all three. To my mind, nature is the totality of reality (the supernatural does not exist), and it exists independently of the spirit, which does not create it but is created by it. It follows, firstly, that everything is immanent to the All (if we may so designate, with a capital letter due to convention rather than deference, the sum total of everything that exists or occurs – Epicurus's *to pan*, Lucretius's *summa summarum*, Spinoza's *Nature*) and, secondly, that nothing can be above or beyond it. That there is only one All is part of the word's definition; if there were several, the All would be their sum. It has no creator; all creators being part of it, they cannot create the All itself. It has no exterior, no exceptions, no purpose other than itself. We can call it reality, namely, all existing entities and events, provided that we include the *ability* to exist and act that makes them possible – the set of causes, not merely the set of effects. It is *physis*, as the Greeks said, rather than *cosmos*, nature rather than the world, process rather than order. It is closer to Lucretius's nature than to Spinoza's – free, yes, but not because it consciously governs itself, only because it is ungoverned by anything outside of itself, at once uncreated and creative, random and necessary, without thought, consciousness or will, without a subject and without an end. All order presupposes it, but none can contain or explain it – *natura sive omnia*, nature, that is, All.

Far from precluding spirituality, this puts spirituality in its place, which may not be first place from the universe's point of view but which is definitely the highest from man's point of view.

I am convinced that nature exists before the spirit that can conceive of it – whence the fact that, to my mind, naturalism leads to materialism. But this does not prevent the spirit from existing; on the contrary, only this can allow it to exist. To be materialistic, in the philosophical sense of the word, is to deny the ontological independence of the spirit. It is not to deny its existence (in which case, materialism itself would become unthinkable). Spirit is not the cause of nature. It is its most interesting, most impressive and most promising effect – for the simple reason that it alone is capable of apprehending interest, impressiveness and promise. Spirituality derives from this and is neither more nor less than what the Scriptures call living 'in spirit and in truth'. What adventure could be more decisive, more precious or more demanding? That spirit is necessarily corporeal is no reason for us to stop using it or to use it only for paltry purposes! Brains are good for far more than studying maps or ordering products on the Internet.

Does the word *absolute* bother you? I understand. I, too, long shied away from it. Indeed, nothing prevents you from replacing it with another. Being? Nature? Becoming? With or without a capital letter? Everyone is free to choose their own vocabulary, and I know of none that are faultless. Still, the word *All* is by definition otherless. On what could it be dependent? To what could it be relative? From where could it be seen? This is what has traditionally been called the absolute or the unconditioned, that which depends on nothing but itself and exists independently of all relations, conditions and points of view. That we have only relative access to it does not prevent it from containing us. That everything contained by the All is relative and conditioned, as I believe to be the case, does not imply that the All itself is relative and conditioned; indeed, if it is truly the All, that possibility is excluded. The sum total of all relations, conditions and points of view is necessarily absolute, unconditioned and invisible. How can it not exist, given that, without it, nothing could exist? This is what I have whimsically dubbed the *panontological* proof: the all of what exists necessarily exists.

Thus, there is nothing contradictory in the notion of a godless spirituality. Westerners are often surprised by this. Since for centuries the only socially observable spirituality in our part of the world has been a religion (Christianity), we have wound up conceiving *religion* and *spirituality* as synonymous. They are not, however! All we need to do is take a few steps – either backwards in time, particularly towards the traditions of Greek philosophy, or sideways in space, towards the Eastern traditions of Buddhism and Taoism, for instance – to discover that there have always existed, and still do exist, forms of spirituality that were or are not religions – at least, not in the Western sense of the word (a belief in one or more gods), and possibly not even in its broader sense (a belief in the sacred or the supernatural). If everything is immanent, then so is the spirit. If everything is natural, then so is spirituality. Far from precluding spiritual life, this makes it possible. We are *in* and *of* the world: spirit is part of nature.

Mysticism and Mystery

Is there such a thing as an atheist spirituality? Thinking back to the three theological virtues of the Christian tradition, I would readily answer that it can be described as a spirituality of fidelity rather than faith, of action rather than hope (yes, action can be a spiritual exercise; such has always been the case with work in Christian monasteries, or, in the

Eastern tradition, with the martial arts) and, naturally, of love rather than fear or submission. The emphasis is placed less on belief than on communion and transmission, less on hope than on action, far less on obedience than on love. These things, however, which were the subject of my first chapter, involve spirituality only in the broadest sense of the term – as a virtual synonym of *ethics* or *wisdom*. They involve not so much our relationship to the absolute, the infinite and the eternal as our relationship to humanity, finitude and time. If we decide to take the word *spirituality* in its more restricted sense, we shall need to go further and higher: at its utmost, spiritual life verges on mysticism.

Here again, it took me a long time to accept the latter word. To my suspicious ears, it had a religious or irrational ring to it. Eventually, however, I was forced to acknowledge that it was the only word that fitted. Reading Wittgenstein's *Tractatus Logico-Philosophicus* made it more palatable to me. The following passage, for instance: 'There is indeed the inexpressible. This *shows* itself; it is the mystical.' That brought mystics closer to me and made Spinoza more comprehensible. More important, it cast a fresh light on my own experience.

For a while, borrowing Martial Guéroult's qualification of Spinoza, I talked about 'mysticism without mystery'. That was my final precaution, but in the end I was forced to throw it, too, to the winds. Not for etymological reasons, of course: though it is true that *mysticism* and *mystery* have the same root word, they are only words, and words prove nothing. The real mystery is not in words but in the world. It is in the spirit, whenever it starts asking questions or looking at reality from a different angle. What is mysterious? Being is mysterious – everything is mysterious! Again, Wittgenstein expresses it perfectly: 'Mysticism wonders not *how* the world is but *that* the world is.' This brings us back to the question of being ('Why is there something rather than nothing?'), except that is no longer a question. Nor is it, quite, an answer. Rather, it is an experience, a sensation, a silence. It can be described as the experience which, in mysticism, corresponds to that question in metaphysics. It is the experience of being, above and beyond the banality of *what is* (as a Heideggerian might put it) – the experience of mystery, above and beyond the apparent self-evidence of explanations.

Most of the time we are oblivious to all this. We are prisoners of the false self-evidence of common awareness, everyday life, routine, 'been there, done that' our claimed or real familiarity with everything – prisoners, in a word, of ideology or habit. 'The world has been disenchanted,' people have been saying since Max Weber. But this is because they forget to look at it or because they have replaced it with a theory. And then, all of a sudden, as you are meditating or walking, you stumble upon this surprise, this revelation, this enchantment, namely, the incredible fact that *there is something, and not nothing*! And the something is why-less, much like Angelus Silesius's rose ('The Rose is without an explanation; She blooms, because She blooms'), since all reasons presuppose its existence – *causa sui*, the philosophers say, 'its own cause'. That names the mystery without dispelling it. In the face of reality, silence is more appropriate. The silence of sensation. The silence of attention. Simone Weil: 'Love and prayer are merely the highest form of attention' – but a prayer that is addressed to no one and asks for nothing. The silence of contemplation. The silence of reality. Such is the spirit of haiku: 'They are wordless, the host, the guest, and the white chrysanthemum.' It is the spirit of Zen masters – 'meditation in silence and with no object'. All that remains is awareness; all that remains is reality. 'Meditation', said Krishnamurti, 'is the silence of thought.' It means, he added, achieving 'freedom from the known' in order to reach reality.

All our explanations are comprised of words; they are derived from the fields of science and philosophy. They should not be renounced (otherwise, would I be writing a book?), but neither should they make us forget the silence they conceal. Far from containing this silence, they are contained by it. It is the silence of that which can be neither explained nor expressed (except indirectly) and which is irreplaceable. All our speeches are about this, which itself is not speech. Not the Word, but silence. Not meaning, but being. This is the field of spirituality or mysticism, when they break free of religion. Being is mystery, not because it is hidden or because it hides something but, on the contrary, because self-evidence and mystery are the same thing, because the mystery is *being* itself.

Immanensity

We are inside, at the very heart of being, the very heart of the mystery. A spirituality of immanence: it is all there, and *it* is what we call the universe.

Is it finite or infinite? We do not know. We cannot know. Even for physicists, the question remains open. And they will never be able to answer it, because they have no way of knowing if our universe is the All – in other words, if the universe they study is the only one there is or if there are others, perhaps even an infinity of universes, in which case the All, which they sometimes call the Multiverse, would be their sum. As for metaphysicists, they have been squabbling about this for centuries. Kant showed it to be one of the insoluble antinomies: when it claims to know the absolute, reason can only fail. Yet the sciences and the universe continue to exist.

From a spiritual point of view, not much is at stake – apart from the fact of our own ignorance, of course. Spirituality has more to do with experience than thought; this is what distinguishes it from metaphysics. And whereas we have a *conception* of the infinite, we have no *experience* of it. We have an experience of the unknown (knowing we do not know), which itself is part of spirituality (the part I have chosen to call mystery). However, we also – and first, and especially – have an experience of immanence and immensity, which, following the poet Jules Laforgue, we can call *immanensity*. We are in the All, and whether it is finite or not, it surpasses us (goes beyond us) in every direction; its limits, if it has any, are permanently beyond our reach. It envelops, contains and exceeds us. Is it a transcendence? Not at all, since we are inside of it. It is an inexhaustible, indefinite immanence, whose limits are both undefined and inaccessible. We are inside it – we live within the unfathomable.

This is something anyone can experience by looking up at the night sky. All you need is a bit of concentration and silence. If the sky is very dark and clear, and you are in the country rather than the city, and you turn out all the lights, look up, and take the time to contemplate in silence . . . Darkness, which separates us from what is close at hand, brings us near to what is far away. You cannot see the far side of your own back garden, but you can see billions of kilometres away with the naked eye. What is that whitish, opalescent streak? The Milky Way, 'our' galaxy, or at least the one to which we belong – some one hundred billion stars, the nearest of which, with the exception of our own sun, is thirty trillion kilometres away. What is that bright dot? Sirius – eight light years (that is, eighty trillion kilometres) away. And what is that barely visible gleam of light over there, near Pegasus's Square? A galaxy known as the Andromeda (there are billions of galaxies, each of them comprising billions of stars), some two million light years or twenty billion billion kilometres away! At night, everything changes scale. As long as the sun was shining, it locked us into the prison of light that is the world – our world. Now, provided there are no clouds, darkness reveals to us the light of the sky, which is the universe. I can barely see the ground beneath my feet, and yet, far better than in broad daylight, I can see the unfathomable that contains me.

True, the experience is a common one, a familiar one. But that only makes it all the more overwhelming, provided you enter into it, give yourself up to it, lose yourself in it. The universe is our home; the celestial vault is our horizon; eternity is here and now. This moves me far more than the Bible or the Koran. It astonishes me far more than miracles (if I believe in them). Compared with the universe, walking on water is a cinch!

Indeed, in the face of such splendour, even believers can scarcely remain indifferent. Pascal expressed it in his own words, with his own sensibility: 'When I consider the short duration of my lifetime, absorbed in the eternity that precedes and follows it, the tiny space I fill and I can even see, lost in the infinite immensity of the spaces of which I know nothing and which know nothing of me, I am dismayed and astonished to find myself here rather than there; for there is no reason to be here rather than there; now rather than then. Who put me here? By whose order and conduct have this place and time been destined for me?'

We can omit the adjective *infinite* from this fragment (the infinite per se can never be the object of experience): this doesn't change the fact that the experience described here is immanence and immensity, and it is this experience, more than anything else, that verges on spirituality. The universe is there; it envelops and exceeds us. It is all; we are next to nothing. To Pascal, this was a source of anxiety. To me, at least when I manage to feel rather than think, it is more like an ocean of peace. 'He who thinks does not perceive,' as the Zen masters say, and 'he who perceives does not think'. We are in the universe, part of the All or of nature. And the contemplation of the immensity that contains us makes us all the more aware of how puny we are. This may be wounding to our ego, but it also enlarges our soul, because the ego has been put in its place at long last. It has stopped taking up all the room.

The argument is a traditional one – but, again, it is less of an argument than an experience: The experience of the immensity of nature is also that of our own puniness. Marcus Aurelius, quoting Plato, used it to keep the fear of death at bay:

> 'Do you think that a man gifted with greatness of
> soul, to whom it is given to contemplate all times
> and all beings, could look upon human existence
> as something great?'
> 'That would be impossible.'
> 'Then he will see nothing awesome in death.'

This goes far beyond the idea of consolation. Marcus Aurelius wanted less to reassure us than to help us grow, less to console us than to set us free. The self is a prison.

To be aware of our own puniness, which in his view is the chief characteristic of 'greatness of soul', is to break free of that prison. This is why sensing nature in all its immensity is a spiritual experience – because it helps the spirit break free, at least partially, of the tiny prison of the self.

Dismay? That is Pascal's word for it. It reflects Pascal's particular sensitivity, which also comes across in another fragment of his *Thoughts*, perhaps one of the most famous, probably one of the most beautiful and definitely the shortest fragment of all: 'The eternal silence of these infinite spaces dismays me.' Is Pascal speaking in his own name here and admitting that he trembles in the dark? Or is he, rather, attributing these words to a freethinker, whom he will then attempt to reassure through religion? The matter has long been debated among commentators. The answer is that there is no way of deciding one way or another, and indeed the two hypotheses are not incompatible. There is something of the proselytizer in Pascal – it is his petty side – but there is also the exceptional mind, one of the greatest ever by its intelligence, its lucidity, its penetration. *That* Pascal speaks to all of us, whether we are believers or not. However, he is a model less for living than for thinking. That his genius was universal does not prevent him from having his own personality, with a marked tendency to anxiety or vertigo. Though it is impossible not to admire him, nothing compels us to imitate him.

To each his own path. Serenity is not my forte, either, but what worries *me* is not the universe – the apparent or actual limitlessness of space, eternity, silence . . . No, what worries me, I readily admit, is everything (that is to say, anything and everything) – everything, that is, *except* the All, which I find soothing. It is a matter of scale, or distance. Virtually all my worries (this is not something of which I'm proud) are egotistical, or at least egocentric ones: I fear only for myself and for those I love; only for myself, my family and friends. This is why the faraway reassures me: it puts my anxieties in perspective. When I contemplate immensity, the ego seems laughable by comparison. It makes my egocentricity, and thus my worries, a little less intense, a little less powerful. Occasionally, it even manages to obliterate them for a few seconds. What a relief, when the ego gets out of the way! Nothing remains but the All, with the body, marvellously, inside of it, as if restored to the world and to itself. Nothing remains but the enormous *thereness* of being, nature and the universe, with no one left inside of us to be dismayed or reassured, or at least no one at this particular instant, in this particular body, to worry about dismay and reassurance, anxiety and danger . . . This is what the Greeks called *ataraxia* (the absence of disturbance) and what the Romans called *pax* (peace, serenity), but in fact it is neither a word (Krishnamurti: 'The word *tranquillity* is not tranquillity') nor a concept. Rather it is an experience, one that involves or passes through the I only to the extent that it breaks free of it.

The ego is perpetually dismayed. Thus, to the extent that the ego separates us from reality, Pascal is right, but whenever the ego temporarily dissolves, he is wrong. The clarity of darkness – 'serene darkness', as Lucretius expressed it – is luminous and kind. How important are our worries compared with the Milky Way? Though the Milky Way cannot dispel our worries (what could?), it can make them more bearable (assuming they are not *too* dreadful), more acceptable (yes, open to observation and action), more ordinary, less weighty . . . The eternal silence of these infinite spaces reassures me.

The Oceanic Feeling

This dissolving of the ego is akin to what Freud, borrowing the expression from novelist Romain Rolland, called 'the oceanic feeling'. He described it as 'a sense of indissoluble union with the great All, and of belonging to the universal', very much as a wave or a drop of water belongs to the ocean. Most of the time, this is indeed no more than a feeling. But occasionally it is an experience, and a powerful one – what contemporary American psychologists call an altered state of consciousness. Of what, exactly, is it an experience? To experience unity, as Swami Prajnanpad would say, is to feel at one with everything.

There is nothing innately religious about the oceanic feeling. Indeed, my own experience of it is quite the opposite. When you feel 'at one with the All', you need nothing more. Why would you need a God? The universe suffices. Why would you need a church? The world suffices. Why would you need faith? Experience suffices.

Of course, when a believer is overcome by the oceanic feeling, it is possible for him or her to describe it in religious terms. It is by no means *necessary*, however. Michel Hulin gives us several descriptions of the state in his fine book on what he calls spontaneous mysticism – that is, the mystical experiences of ordinary individuals who have not been classified as mystics in the traditional sense of the term. These accounts, while they come from individuals who differ from one another in many ways (some are believers, others not), are generally convergent. They describe the same suddenness, the same sense of 'everything being there', the same presence of eternity, the same fullness, the same silence ('the intellect is disconnected', as Hulin puts it), the same unspeakable, overabundant joy . . . Hulin quotes the following passage from Marius Favre, for instance: 'Had I been absorbed by the universe, or had the universe penetrated me? These expressions had become virtually meaningless, since the border between my body and the world had vanished – or rather, seemed to have been neither more nor less than hallucination of my reason, not melting in the flame of truth . . . Everything was there, more present than ever before . . .' Or the following passage from Richard Jefferies: 'Eternity is here and now. I am within it. It is all around me in the brightness of the sun. I am within it, much like a butterfly floating on the light-permeated air. Nothing is still to come. Everything is already here. Eternity now. Immortal life now. I am experiencing it here, at this very instant, as I stand next to this mound . . .' Or again, from Margaret Montague: 'I saw nothing that was new, but I saw all the usual things in a new and miraculous light – in what I believe to be their true light. I perceived the extravagant splendour, the indescribable joy of life in its totality. Every person walking across the veranda, every sparrow in flight, every tiny branch waving in the wind was an integral part of the whole, and seemed to be taking part in this mad ecstasy of joy, meaning, and inebriated life. I saw that this beauty was everywhere present . . . Once, at least, amidst the drabness of the days of my life, I will have seen into the heart of reality and been witness to the truth.' Reading these descriptions, who could possibly say whether their authors believed in God or not? The experiences they describe involve no particular theology or belief; they make no attempt to confirm or refute dogma. This is just why they are so powerful – because they evoke something each and all of us can experience, regardless of our religious or irreligious convictions.

Indeed, there is another text, one not quoted by Hulin but one that, though situated in a clearly atheistic spiritual climate, seems to me very analogous. True, it is from a novel, but I am fairly certain that its author, independently of the story he was telling, was writing out of personal experience. The text to which I'm referring is the final passage of Albert Camus's *The Stranger*. We are in the mind of a man who has been condemned to death, on the eve of his execution: 'The exquisite peace of this sleepy summer flowed into me like a tide . . . Emptied of hope, as I stood there staring at the night sky filled with signs and stars, I opened myself up to the tender indifference of the universe for the first time. Feeling it so like myself, so fraternal at long last, I realized that I had been happy, and still was.' This celebration of a 'wedding with the world', as Camus describes it elsewhere, is definitely part of a spiritual experience, but one that is entirely immanent. It involves neither hope nor belief. To call it happiness would be either too much or not enough, for it is an experience that goes beyond the framework of ordinary human psychology. It is as if truth coincided at last with the world and our awareness of it. 'When am I more true than when I am the world?' asked Camus in *The Wrong Side and the Right Side* and by way of an answer, he added, 'I am fulfilled even before I can long for anything. Eternity is here and I was hoping for it. What I wish for now is no longer to be happy, but only to be aware.' Is this absurd? That is not the question, for the simple reason that all questions have vanished. The absurd is merely a starting point; in Camus, it can lead to either a politics of revolt or an ethics of love, but it can also (and perhaps especially) lead to a mysticism of silence and immanence.

The fact that people have had this sort of experience on every continent, in widely diverging intellectual and spiritual contexts, only makes the resemblance among their descriptions all the more striking. The oceanic feeling belongs to no religion or philosophy in particular, and this is a good thing. It is neither a dogma nor an act of faith; it is an experience.

Freud responded with perplexity to Romain Rolland's account of this state, which is frequently described as a form of revelation. Freud, who is known to have been anything but a mystic, admitted to never having felt such a thing. It is difficult not to hear accents of regret in the following passage from his July 1929 letter to Rolland: 'The worlds you are exploring are utterly foreign to me! Mysticism is as inaccessible to me as music.' This was probably why he attached so much importance to his 'venerated friend's' description. Being what he was, however, Freud went on to interpret it in psychoanalytic terms, if only to put it at a distance – or, as he himself phrased it, to 'remove it from my path'. Such was his intent in the opening pages of *Civilization and Its Discontents*. Freud saw the oceanic feeling as the expression of a 'limitless narcissism', which he attributed to a 'primitive phase of the sense of self' – anterior, in small babies, to the split between the self and the outside world. Well, maybe. This might explain why so many people, in describing this state, have evoked the experience of love, in the sense of love received rather than felt or given. Is it self-love? Mother love? A regression to the womb? A narcissistic projection? Anything is possible, and nothing is certain. Personally (since in matters such as these each of us can speak only for him- or herself), I have experienced nothing of the sort. I have always felt the universe to be indifferent to everything (that is, to itself) – neither loving nor unloving, utterly devoid of affect. That *I* can love *it* is a good thing – indeed, the best there is. But why should *it* love *me*? Nature is not our mother, fortunately enough. One mother per lifetime is quite sufficient.

Yet the oceanic feeling, as Rolland or Freud describes it, is not unknown to me. Yes, like countless others, I have experienced what Freud called 'that sense of eternity, of something limitless, something with no borders', that sense of total security, even in the face of danger, the certainty that 'you cannot fall out of the universe', the sense of being 'at one with the All' . . . and never have I experienced anything more powerful, more delightful, more overwhelming or more soothing. Was it ecstasy? I wouldn't call it that, because there was no exterior to float away to. Instead, I would call it *enstasy* – the experience of an interiority (but one that contained me, rather than my containing it), an immanence, a unity, an immersion, an insideness. Was it a vision? No, at least not in the usual sense of the term. Never have I felt anything more natural. Was it a mystery? Yes, perhaps, but a self-evident one. Was it a revelation? If you like, but one that contained neither a message nor a secret.

A Mystical Experience

The first time it happened, I was in a forest in the north of France. I must have been twenty-five or twenty-six. I had just been hired to teach high-school philosophy in a town on the edge of a canal, up in the fields near the Belgian border. That particular evening, some friends and I had gone out for a walk in the forest we liked so much. Night had fallen. We were walking. Gradually our laughter faded, and the conversation died down. Nothing remained but our friendship, our mutual trust and shared presence, the mildness of the night air and of everything around us . . . My mind empty of thought, I was simply registering the world around me – the darkness of the undergrowth, the incredible luminosity of the sky, the faint sounds of the forest (branches snapping, an occasional animal call, our own muffled steps) only making the silence more palpable. And then, all of a sudden . . . What? Nothing: everything! No words, no meanings, no questions, only – a surprise. Only – this. A seemingly infinite happiness. A seemingly eternal sense of peace. Above me, the starry sky was immense, luminous and unfathomable, and within me there was nothing but the sky, of which I was a part, and the silence, and the light, like a warm hum, and a sense of joy with neither subject nor object (no object other than everything, no subject other than itself). Yes, in the darkness of that night, I contained only the dazzling presence of the All. Peace. Infinite peace! Simplicity, serenity, delight.

The two latter words may sound incompatible, but at the time they weren't words, they were experience: silence, harmony. It was as if a perfect chord, once played, had been indefinitely prolonged, and that chord was the world. I felt fine. Incredibly fine! So fine that I didn't even need to notice it or hope that it would last. I can scarcely even say that *I* was walking – the walk was there, and the forest, and the trees and our group of friends . . . The *ego* had vanished: no more separation or representation, only the silent *presentation* of everything. No more value judgements; only reality. No more time; only the present. No more nothingness; only being. No more frustration, hatred, fear, anger or anxiety; only joy and peace. No more make-believe, illusions, lies; only the truth, which I did not contain but which contained me. It may have lasted only a few seconds. I felt at once stunned and reconciled, stunned and calmer than I'd ever felt before. I had a sense of detachment, freedom and necessity, as if the universe had been restored to itself at long last. Was it finite or infinite? That was not the question. There *were* no more questions, so how could there be answers? There was only self-evidence. And silence. And the truth – but without words. And the world – but without signification or purpose. And imma-nence – but without its opposite. And reality – but without otherness. There was no faith, no hope, no sense of promise. There was only everything – the beauty, truth and presence of everything. This was enough. It was far more than enough! A sense of joyous acceptance. A sense of dynamic quietude – yes, like an unlimited courage. Rest without fatigue. What was death? Nothing. What was life? Only this palpitation of being within me. What was salvation? Only a word, or else this state itself. Perfection. Plenitude. Bliss. Such joy! Such happiness! Such intensity!

'This is what Spinoza meant by eternity,' I said to myself – and, naturally, that put an end to it, or expelled me from it. Words returned, and thought, and the ego, and separation. But it didn't matter; the universe was still there, and I was there with it, or within it. How can you fall out of the All? How can eternity come to an end? How can words stifle silence? I had experienced a moment of perfection, a moment of bliss – just long enough to realize what these things were.

'We sense and experience that we are eternal,' wrote Spinoza in his *Ethics*. Not that we *shall* be eternal, after death, but that we *are* eternal, here and now. This, indeed, was what I had just sensed and experienced. It was much like a revelation, but without God. Not only was it the most beautiful moment of my life, it was also the most joyous, the most serene, and the most clearly spiritual one. How pale and wan the prayers of my childhood or my adolescence seemed by contrast! Too many words. Too much ego. Too much narcissism. What I felt that night – and have felt or come close to feeling on a few other occasions – was virtually the opposite. It was like truth without words, consciousness without ego, happiness without narcissism. Intellectually, of course, it proved nothing, yet I could not pretend it hadn't happened.

When I caught up with my friends, who had got a little ahead of me, I said nothing to them of what I had just experienced. It was time to go home. My life resumed – or, rather, continued to follow – its usual course. I let eternity go on without me. I'm not the sort of person who can live in the absolute on a long-term basis – but, for the space of a few seconds, the absolute had lived in me. At last I had understood the meaning of salvation – or bliss, or eternity; the word matters little, since it was not a verbal event. I had felt it, *experienced* it, so now I could dispense with having to look for it.

I have experienced similar moments over the years, less and less frequently as time went on, though this did not particularly bother me. A few years later, I came to understand that if great mystics are usually childless, it is because children – through an excess of love, passion, anxiety, worry – attach us to reality and thus separate us from the absolute, or at least prevent us from inhabiting it simply. Indeed, I would say that these moments permanently modified my relationship to time; they calmed it down (yes, within the maelstrom of anxiety); they purified and liberated it. They taught me to be more open to the present, to the way time passes and the way it lingers, to the eternity of becoming, to the perpetual impermanence of everything . . . Though few and far between, these experiences have changed my daily life, making it a bit less heavy – and even, on good days, happier. They have lastingly transformed my relationship to the world, to other people, to myself, to art (there is such eternity, sometimes, in Vermeer or in Mozart!), to philosophy, to spirituality . . . I have never thought of myself as a mystic, still less a sage. I have spent more time thinking about eternity (writing commentaries, for instance, on the fifth book of Spinoza's *Ethics*) than living it. Whether I like it or not, that is what it means to be a philosopher. But now, at least I had some idea what I was talking about – first in my classes and later in my own books. I now had an inkling of what Epicurus, Spinoza and Wittgenstein meant when they referred, respectively, to 'immortal goods', '*sub specie aeternitatis*' and 'endless' life. Though I hadn't read them yet, I also knew what Lao-tzu, Nagarjuna, Krishnamurti, Prajnanpad and the sages of virtually all countries, languages and traditions were talking about – and I knew that it was a matter, not of words, but of silence.

Is It Possible to Speak About Silence?

Notwithstanding Lao-tzu and Wittgenstein – or, rather, along with these thinkers – we must try to say something about silence.

'The Tao that can be expressed is not the Tao of all time,' said Lao-tzu. Of course this is true, since *Tao* is merely a name, whereas the Tao (the absolute) is nameless. All the more reason, as the *Tao Te Ching* demonstrates, to attempt to express – inevitably in words – something that is neither speech nor written words.

'Whereof one cannot speak,' said Wittgenstein, 'thereof one must be silent.' True enough. But *what* cannot be spoken about? That an object is silent does not make it inexpressible. That stones cannot talk does not prevent us from saying true things about them. All sensation is mute (*alogos*, as Epicurus said), yet our words not only depend upon but proceed from it. The fact that the truth is not a statement does not prevent certain statements from being true.

Indeed, even if the absolute were inexpressible, the same would not be true of all experiences that aim at or encounter the absolute. Look at poets, artists, mystics: why shouldn't philosophers follow their lead? How, indeed, can they avoid doing so? Thinking through human experience in its entirety, as it is incumbent upon them to do, also implies thinking through, however imperfectly, our relationship to the absolute. Can we express the inexpressible? It may be that we have never expressed anything else. Can we talk about silence? Why not? Far better to do that than talk only about speech.

'The idea of a circle is not round,' said Spinoza, 'and the concept of a dog does not bark.' Similarly, the concept of silence is not silent, any more than the concept of the absolute is absolute. This is what enables us to talk about the things themselves (rather than merely the concepts of these things) – using words, of course, and relatively. This is no more contradictory than making statements about dogs that are not made up of barks. Whereof one can remain silent, and only thereof can one speak.

So let us try to do so.

In retrospect, if I attempt to draw a few conclusions from what I learned during those rare experiences, and also from the books I have read on the subject, written either by mystics (generally from the East) or by philosophers (generally from the West), it seems to me that the modified state of consciousness characteristic of the mystical experience results from a number of temporary suspensions. I have already mentioned several of them in passing, but it is no doubt useful at this point to draw up a list that is at once succinct and fairly exhaustive.

Mystery and Self-evidence

Firstly . . . but the word *firstly* applies only to the present evocation, which is necessarily successive, not to the experience itself, which is innately simultaneous. Firstly, there is the suspension of familiarity, banality, repetition, 'been there done that' – the spurious self-evidence of ordinary awareness. All at once, it is as if everything were new, singular and astonishing – not irrational, perhaps, but inexplicable or incomprehensible, beyond all forms of reason. Given that reason is a part of it, how could reason possibly contain it? This is what I call *mystery*.

Secondly, or rather at the same time, there is the suspension of questions and problems – not because they have all been resolved, but because they are simply no longer raised. Why is there something rather than nothing? The question vanishes and all that remains is the answer, which is no longer an answer, since there is no longer a question. All that remains is being, reality, what I have called *self-evidence*. Woody Allen comes close to it in one of his aphorisms: 'The answer is yes. But what is the question?' There *is* no question, which is why the answer is always yes. And yes is not so much an answer as it is an acknowledgement within ourselves of the presence (of everything). Being is at once a mystery and a fact; the two are one and the same thing. This is why the mystery is no more a problem than the self-evidence is a solution. Wittgenstein put it most aptly: 'For an answer which cannot be expressed, the question too cannot be expressed . . . The solution to the problem of life is seen in the vanishing of the problem.'

Mystery and self-evidence are one and the same thing – that is, the world. The mystery of being is the light of being.

Plenitude

Another thing that is suspended in these moments is lack. This is an utterly unique sensation. We spend most of our time running after things we do not possess, things we consider to be missing and wish to procure for ourselves. Lucretius was well aware of this:

> Whilst the thing we long for
> Is lacking, that seems good above all else;
> Thereafter, when we've touched it, something else
> We long for; ever one equal thirst of life
> Grips us agape.
>
> —trans. William Ellery Leonard

We are prisoners of lack, prisoners of nothingness. Are we prisoners of our desires? Of *thirst*, says Lucretius, and

Buddha agrees with him (*tanhā*); of *hope*, say the Stoics, the wish for what we do not possess. We do not live, we hope to live, as Pascal puts it, following Seneca. Nothingness clings to us because we cling to it.

Yet there are the occasional moments of grace, when we cease hoping for anything other than what is (and this is no longer hope; it is love) or what we are doing (and this is no longer hope; it is will). Moments when nothing is missing, when there is nothing to either wish for or regret and when the question of possession is irrelevant (because having is replaced by being and doing) – this is what I call *plenitude*. To achieve it, one need not spend endless hours meditating, though it might help. Is there such a thing as a person who has never experienced a moment of plenitude? It can be in sex, when you stop pursuing performance or the other person or yourself, and when even orgasm and love are no longer lacking, when all that remains is pure pleasure, as Lucretius says, *pura voluptas*, pure desire, but without lack, the pure ability to achieve and give bliss; or in sports, the miracle of second wind, when all that remains is the pure ability to run; or in communion with a work of art (how fulfilling it can be to listen to Mozart!); or in a sublime landscape (who would want to *own* the Alps or the Atlantic Ocean?); or again, more simply and more peacefully, in the course of a walk or a hike . . .

You are taking a walk in the country. You feel great. It started out as an activity for recreation or exercise – a few hours to kill, a few ounces to work off . . . And then it gradually turned into something else – a subtler, deeper, nobler pleasure. Something like an adventure, but an interior one. Or like an experience, but a spiritual one. Who cares about those extra ounces? Who cares about boredom or anxiety? You no longer have a goal, or else you have already reached it. More accurately still, you reach it anew with every passing second: you are walking. It is like a pilgrimage through immanence, but a pilgrimage that takes you nowhere or takes you only exactly where you are. You wish for nothing other than the step you are taking at the very moment you take it, nothing other than the landscape as it is, at this very instant, with a bird emitting its cry, another bird taking wing, the strength you feel in your calves, the lightness in your heart and the peace in your soul . . . And since you are indeed taking that step, since the landscape is as it is, since one bird does cry and the other does take wing, since you are exactly what you are (dynamic, joyful, serene), you lack nothing: this is plenitude.

The mystical experience merely goes a bit further in the same direction: what fulfils you then is not a particular state of being but being itself. All at once, you find yourself miraculously free of frustration – free of lack, free of nothingness! All that remains is being; all that remains is joy. Anguish is the perception of nothingness; joy is the perception of being. All that remains is the fullness of reality. How could you yearn for anything else? Within you, there are no more lacks to be filled. Is this because you have everything? No, it is because you have been freed from possession itself (and this is where it verges on spirituality). All that remains is being without belonging – and, within you, the joy of being part of it.

The ego is perpetually frustrated. When frustration vanishes, so does the ego.

Simplicity

This is also why you are freed of yourself – because there is no longer a split between the you who does and the you who observes the doing, between soul and body, between *I* and *me*. All that remains is the *I*. All that remains is consciousness. All that remains is action – the body in action. Inner duality has been suspended. So has representation, the whole theatre of the *me*. The ego is placed in parentheses. This is what I call *simplicity*. You stop pretending to be what you are (thus, simplicity is the very opposite of bad faith, in the Sartrean sense of the term), without trying to be something else (thus, simplicity is a challenge to existentialism). Go ahead, right this minute: *try* not to be what you are or to be what you are not! Indeed, you are nothing – at least, you are neither a being nor a substance. You live, feel, act. There is only a 'flood of perceptions' (Hume), an action without an actor, a life with no subject apart from itself. There is only, Wittgenstein would say, an experience ('All experience is of the world and has no need of a subject'). This is what Buddhists call *anatman*, no-me, no-self, nothing but a subjectless, goalless process. Despite the word's initial letter, which means 'without', it is not experienced as a negation or a deprivation. This is why I prefer to call it simplicity rather than nonself or nonego. From a metaphysical point of view, nothing is more difficult to describe (cf. Spinoza, Hume, Nietzsche, Lévi-Strauss). From a spiritual point of view, nothing is easier to experience, even if it remains exceptional. These are the moments in which we 'forget ourselves', as the saying goes, and never is our consciousness as pure, as sharp or as agile as it is then. In concerts, virtuosi – at least the greatest among them – sometimes achieve this state. These are their moments of grace, when all that remains is the music. All of us, however, are capable of achieving it according to our degree of simplicity, mastery and virtuosity in one field or another. Simplicity of action. Simplicity of attention. 'When you are absorbed in an activity, no matter what it is, can you feel any self at all?' asks Prajnanpad. 'No, the separation has disappeared.' This is because all that remains is the activity.

Those who watch themselves act are not involved in true action. Those who try to be attentive are not involved in true attention.

Do you find it difficult to be simple? Start off with what comes most easily to you – sitting, walking, breathing . . . Such is the spirit of Soto Zen: 'The technique is the path; the path is the technique.' But the place to which the path takes you is no longer a technique or a path. It is life itself, in all its simplicity. Instead of looking at yourself, you can see. Instead of pretending, you can act. Instead of waiting, you can pay attention. What could be simpler than simplicity? And what could be rarer? It means being at one with yourself, so much so that the self vanishes, and all that remains is oneness – the act itself, awareness itself. You were taking a walk? All that remains is the walk. You were making love? All that remains is desire or love. You were meditating? All that remains is meditation. You were acting? All that remains is action – such is the secret of martial arts, which is why they involve spirituality. You were being? All that remains is being itself.

Unity

Thus, the gap between you and yourself has closed. But so has the gap between you and the world, between inside and outside, between the *I* and everything else. Duality has been suspended or bracketed – but so, therefore, has the ego; all that remains is everything, and the unity of all things. This, again, is what Freud and Rolland called the oceanic feeling, what Eastern thought calls *advaita* (nonduality or nondualism) and what, following Swami Prajnanpad, I prefer to call the experience of *unity*. It is indissociable from the experience of simplicity – so much so, indeed, that it is hard to distinguish between the two, even conceptually. When inner duality vanishes, so does the duality between one's self and the outside world. If we are at one with our consciousness or our body (and the two go together in what I call simplicity), we will also be at one with the world (in what I call unity). 'In truth, there is only one, with no second,' as Prajnanpad accurately put it.

Philosophically, and thus in retrospect, it is not unlike the tenets of monism or pantheism. We can see it as being reminiscent of Spinoza's unity of substance or the materialists' material unity of the world. It is the opposite of systems based on exclusion, for it is an experience that resembles an immersion, a fusion, a successful integration. It is not a matter of being Spinozist or materialist; it is a matter of being at one with the All.

All egos are separate by definition. When separation ends, so does the ego.

'I am the world,' was Krishnamurti's way of putting it. And here, perhaps even more apt, is Prajnanpad's: 'Swami is going to tell you a secret. Swami knows one and only one thing – that he is at one with the all.' This is the wisdom of immanence, the mysticism of unity.

Silence

The same spiritual experience puts brackets around language, discourse and reason – what the Greeks called *logos* and Easterners call *manas* or *intellect*. We are separated from the all only by thought, only by ourselves. When the ego is relinquished, when thought ceases, the all remains.

Is this aphasia? Is it speechlessness? By no means, at least not in the pathological sense of the term. Thought remains possible. Speech remains possible. They have simply ceased to be necessary. There is a suspension, as it were, of interior monologue, argumentative or conceptual thought, meaning – and also, therefore, of nonmeaning, or the absurd. All that remains is reality. All that remains is sensation, which is part of reality. It is like seeing things for what they are at last, without masks, labels or names. Usually this is not the case: we are almost always separated from the world by the very words that serve to express it or protect us from it (interpretation, rationalization, justification). And then, all of a sudden, in the midst of a meditation, a sensation or an act – truth itself, but wordless truth. *Alogos* was Epicurus's word for it. *Aphasia* was Pyrrhus's (not the impossibility of speech but its at least temporary suspension). This is what I call *silence*. It is the absence, not of noise, but of words – not of sound, but of sense. The silence of the sea. The silence of the wind. The silence of wise people, even when they speak.

It is hardly necessary to add that this suspension of reason (of *our* reason) is not itself irrational, any more than Spinoza's 'third type of knowledge', which perhaps corresponds to it, is irrational. Silence is what remains when we cease talking – that is, everything. It leaves the truth intact. Simply, this truth 'has no need of a sign', as Spinoza said, and signifies nothing. Rather than asking to be interpreted, it asks to be known or contemplated. It is not a representation but 'the objective essence of things' (Spinoza), what a Buddhist would call their simple, wordless *thusness*. What we talk about (reality) is not a discourse. Nor is what we say (the truth). We are separated from these things only by our lies and illusions. We need only stop talking, or rather create silence within ourselves (to stop talking is easy; to create silence, far more difficult), and nothing will remain but the truth, which all discourses presuppose, which contains them all, but which can be contained by none. The truth of silence: the silence of truth.

Eternity

There is something even more amazing and even more powerful. What occurs in the experience I am describing is also, and perhaps especially, the suspension of time, or rather what we habitually think of as time. Actual time continues, of course. The present continues. Duration continues. That, indeed, is all that remains. For what you then notice in yourself is something like a setting aside of past and future – of what phenomenologists call *temporality*, what the Stoics call *aion* (the indefinite and noncorporeal sum of a past that no longer exists and a future that does not yet exist, separated by an instant without duration), and what, borrowing poet Jules Laforgue's delightful neologism, I would readily call *eternullity*. This eternity that is nothing, or next to nothing, this endless nullity, this endlessness that imprisons us is what we generally experience as the 'flight' of time, the irreversible, unstoppable engulfment of the future, which is not yet, by the past, which is no more. What separates the two? The present instant, which is nothing and has no duration. If it had a specific duration, it would be neither the instant nor the present. Part of it would be past and the rest yet to come. A quasi-nonentity, therefore, squashed between two nonentities – that time which, as Montaigne rightly observed, ordinarily separates us from being and eternity. And then, all of a sudden – no more past! No more future! Nothing but the present, which remains present. Nothing but eternity.

Conceptually (and thus in retrospect), this is comprehensible. The past does not exist, since it is no more. The future does not exist, since it is not yet. Thus, there is only the present, which changes at every instant, but continues and remains present. Who has ever experienced a single yesterday? Who has ever experienced a single tomorrow? It is always today. It is always now. 'Only the present exists,' the Stoics rightly said, and therefore 'all time is present'. But it is no longer *aion*, that abstract time that we can divide up and measure, waste and be wasted by. Rather it is *chronos*, a concrete time that is the universe's present, the universe as presence – what Spinoza and Bergson called duration, the indefinite and indivisible pursuance of an existence. Just try to measure or divide up the present! You will not succeed, for it is not *a* duration. It is duration itself, for as long as it lasts. Not a lapse of time, but time itself. This time does not move towards us from the future, which is nothing, nor is it engulfed by the past, which is no more. Not coincidentally, we can say of it what Parmenides said of being: 'It neither was nor shall be, because it is.'

Now, a present that remains present is exactly what has traditionally been called *eternity* – not an infinite length of time, which it would be more accurate to call *sempiternity*, but what Saint Augustine called an 'eternal present', God's 'perpetual today', but which I myself would call the perpetual today of the universe (the ever-presentness of the real) and of truth (the ever-presentness of the true), which, in the present, are one and the same thing, namely eternity.

Yes, all of this can be understood *in retrospect*, but then we are no longer living it. While we are living it, it is neither a concept, a reflection nor a comprehension. It is an experience. It is a fact. It is a bedazzlement. The present is here, and it is all there is. It never vanishes; it continues. It changes ceaselessly; therefore it is unceasing. All is present; the present is all. All is true. All is eternal, here and now! This is the meaning of Spinoza's amazing statement, already quoted above: 'We sense and experience that we are eternal.' Wittgenstein grasped the same thing: 'If by eternity we mean not infinite duration but intemporality, then he who lives in the present has eternal life.' It is only natural that at such times even death should be indifferent to him. He is already saved – or, more accurately, there is no 'he' left to save; there is only ever-present eternity, eternity in action. How pitiful heaven seems by contrast! How could eternity be in the future? How could we wait for it or yearn to reach it, since we are in it already?

Eternity of the present; presence of eternity.

Serenity

This leaves us nothing to hope for and nothing to fear. Both hope and fear are suspended, as are expectation, anticipation and *worry* about 'futureness', as Heidegger said, or as his translators quote him as saying. Worry is an intrinsic part of *Dasein*: it is the ego's being-before-itself, which, in Heidegger's terms, condemns us to being-for-death. How could we *not* be worried? Such is the price to pay for nothingness, futureness and the ego.

But what if nothingness does not exist? What if the ego does not exist? What if only the present exists? Then all that remains is serenity, which is the being-in-the-present of awareness and the all.

Carpe diem? That expression derives from wisdom (and a rather pat wisdom at that), not spirituality. *Carpe aeternitatem* would be more like it, except that there is nothing to seize and everything to contemplate.

It is reminiscent of what Stoicism and other forms of wisdom have called 'living in the present' – except that, in this case, it is no longer a motto or an ideal. Rather, it is the simple truth of life.

Just try to live in the past or the future. You will realize at once that it is impossible, and that the present is the only path. Memories, plans, dreams? Either they are present or else they do not exist. Thus, the present is not something you can choose, since choice itself exists only in the present. It is something you can inhabit.

It is also reminiscent of what I referred to above as cheerful despair – except that there is nothing despairing about it, and even the word 'cheerful' has a superficial or trivial ring to it when applied to this experience. Rather, it is a voyage to the far side of despair, where both sides are as one.

In Greek, as I have already noted, this state was called *ataraxia*, the absence of disturbance; in Latin it was called *pax*, peace. In English, it might be called *tranquillity* or *serenity*. Not for nothing is there quietism in all forms of mysticism. Look at Fénelon or Chuang-tzu. Taoism, as ethnologist Marcel Granet said, is a 'wisdom with mystical overtones', 'a sort of naturalistic quietism'. This has nothing to do with laziness or idleness, and still less with spinelessness! Simply, hope and fear go hand in hand – I have already quoted Spinoza's incisive phrase: 'There is no hope without fear, and no fear without hope' – so, therefore, do the absence of one and the other. For all that, it is not an absence; it is a presence, an attentiveness, an availability. Nothing to hope for, nothing to fear – everything is here. This is what the experience I am describing brings about. What peace! What tranquillity! Hopelessness? It might seem that way, but only from the outside, or on the way there. From the inside, it is more like an *unhope*, the zero degree of hope and fear. It is more like happiness – Krishnamurti: 'To live happily is to live without hope.' Spinoza gave it its true name: *beatitude*.

We can hope only for what we do not have, what we are not or what we lack. With rare exceptions, we can hope only for the future, whereas we can live only in the present. 'Hope is humankind's greatest enemy,' said Prajnanpad; serenity is its greatest victory. It means freeing ourselves of fear – so much so that, in the state I am describing, even courage is no longer necessary.

The objection might be raised that this puts an end to politics. Not at all (cf. Spinoza). It does, however, prevent politics from posing as mysticism, just as it prevents mysticism from posing as politics. This is a good thing. The absolute is not a form of government. No government can be the absolute – hence the importance of separating church from state.

Serenity is not inactivity. Rather, it is activity without fear and thus, also, without hopefulness. Why not? What stirs us to action, as I said in the first chapter, is not hopefulness but will. What makes us want something is not hopefulness but desire or love. There is no escaping reality. There is no escaping the present. Such is the spirit of the martial arts. Those who hope for victory are already vanquished, if only by their fear of defeat. Only those who hope for nothing can be fearless. This, indeed, is what makes them difficult to overcome and impossible to force into submission. They can be derived of victory, but not of their combat.

Action is a part of the very reality it transforms, just as the wave is a part of the ocean. The point is not to renounce action, but to act with serenity. Our action will be all the more effective, and all the happier.

This is what I call happiness in action, which is the same thing as perceiving action itself as happiness. If you live in the present and lack nothing, what could you hope for? What could you fear? Reality – of which action is a part – is utterly sufficient and utterly fulfilling.

Acceptance

Because all is well? No, because well *is*. This is the hardest thing of all to conceptualize. The experience I am trying to describe also implies the suspension of value judgements, the setting aside of ideals and norms – beauty and ugliness, for instance, or good and evil, or justice and injustice. Wittgenstein came close to expressing this when he wrote, in his *Notebooks* rather than his *Tractatus*, 'Everything that happens, whether caused by a stone or by my own body, is neither good nor bad.' This does not preclude joy. It does not preclude happiness. Indeed, it is happiness itself – as long as it is present. Again in his *Notebooks*, Wittgenstein said, 'I am happy or unhappy; that is all. We can say: there is neither good nor evil.' There is only reality, which has no other. To what norms or rules could it be subjected?

Does this endorse immorality? Not at all. Morality is a part of reality; what prevents it from having absolute value is just what prevents us from abolishing it. What it does endorse is *amorality*, both theoretically (for thought) and contemplatively (for spirituality). Spinoza expressed this with his usual rigour: 'Good and evil do not exist in Nature,' and nothing exists outside of Nature. Hence, reality and perfection are one and the same thing – not because all is well, as the providentialists would have it, but because good and evil do not exist. This by no means prevents us from constructing an ethics (things can be good or bad *for us*) or even from conceiving a morality, which entails the at once illusory and necessary absolutization of ethics. It does, on the other hand, prevent us from turning it into a metaphysics or an ontology – projecting on to Nature, in other words, what exists only within ourselves, mistaking our judgements for knowledge, our ideals for reality, and thus, especially, mistaking reality, when it doesn't correspond to our ideals, for an offence or a degeneration. Evil is nothing, as Gilles Deleuze said in his writings on Spinoza, not 'because only Good can exist and cause to exist', as the theologians would have it, 'but on the contrary because neither good nor evil exist, and because existence is beyond good and evil'.

It might be objected that this defeats one of the arguments against God discussed above ('the argument of evil'). Not really, since evil continues to exist *for subjects*, and God is assumed to be a subject. What it does do is remove all reasons for belief. Reality suffices. Why subject it to anything else? All is perfect. Thus, we no longer need consolation, hope or a last judgement; the point is less to judge than to understand, and less to understand than to see. Reality: take it or leave it. Or rather, in the experience

I am describing: reality is that which can only be taken, since it is itself its own taking, and the rest falls away of its own accord.

This is what Nietzsche, in response and partly in opposition to the Stoics, called *amor fati*, love of fate, loving what is – not because it is good (indeed, to Nietzsche's mind, fate was the very opposite of providence), but because it is the set of all things that occur (the universe, reality), and because nothing else exists. It is the one-with-no-second in the Nietzschean manner, or what Clément Rosset described as reality with no duplicate and no remedy. You can take it or leave it, I said. Ascetics leave it. Wise men take it.

As Nietzsche pointed out, this is a tragic wisdom: 'The Dionysiac affirmation of the universe as it is, with no possibility of subtraction, exception or choice'. It means participating in the 'innocence of becoming', the 'eternal yes of being', which is the self-affirmation of all.

Prajnanpad called it the wisdom of acceptance. 'No denial' – that is, neither rejection nor refusal. 'Not what should be, but what is' – neither hope nor regret. It is the only path: 'There is no way out except acceptance.' We must say yes to all that is and to all that occurs, but it is the yes of acceptance (all is true, all is real), not the yes of approval (all is well). It is the yes of wisdom, not of religion – or, more accurately, it is not a word, and neither wisdom nor religion exists. All that exists is the eternal necessity of becoming, which is true being.

To judge is to compare, and there is no denying that this is something we are often required to do in everyday life. It is the very principle of morality and politics, and naturally we must renounce neither of these things. It is also the principle of art, and we must not renounce that, either. How could morality exist without refusal? How could politics exist without confrontation? How could art exist without evaluation and criticism, revision and hierarchy? The mystical state, however, enables us to experience something else, namely that reality is exactly what it is – that it has no defects, that it can neither be compared to anything else, since it is all, nor, therefore, judged, since all judgements are part of it. In this sense, it is *perfect*. This is the meaning of Spinoza's 'By reality and perfection I mean the same thing', Nietzsche's *Beyond Good and Evil* or – perhaps the aptest way of putting it – Prajnanpad's *neutrality*. To understand the latter term, we must briefly evoke its context. One of the swami's disciples asked him about the meaning of the famous Upanishad phrase 'All is Brahman', which has often been translated as 'All is God' or 'All is the Absolute'. Prajnanpad replied simply, 'Everything is neutral.' This is what I call relativism – or, more accurately, it is the positive reverse of relativism: only reality is absolute; all value judgements are relative.

It is the opposite of a theodicy. We are saying, not that all is well in this best of all possible worlds, but that all is as it is in the only real world, which is the world.

It is also the opposite of nihilism. We are not proposing

to abolish morality. To say yes to everything is also to say yes to our value judgements, our refusals and revolts, which are part of the all. Simply, we acknowledge that morals are only human. They are *our* morals, not those of the universe or the absolute. The same goes for politics: the fact that the absolute is apolitical, neither left- nor right-wing, by no means eliminates politics. On the contrary! It is just because the universe has no political position, since it contains them all, that we ourselves are obliged to choose one. Politics cannot be part of the mystical experience, but this only confirms that mysticism does not cover everything. Again, the separation of church and state is crucial. We mustn't count on the absolute to combat injustice for us. Nor, on the other hand, must we count on politics to replace spirituality.

Finally, it is the opposite of aestheticism. Beauty is something we can create or love – fine. Art exists – so much the better! But it would be wrong to turn it into a mysticism or a religion. Beauty can give us access to the absolute, but it is not itself the absolute. From a spiritual point of view, what matters is not whether or not we create a work of art, still less whether or not we turn our lives into a work of art. On this subject, Chuang-tzu is more enlightening than the Romantics: 'The perfect man is without a self, the inspired man is without works; the saintly man leaves no name behind him.' This takes nothing away from a genius (except his vanity, if he was vain); it does, however, put him in his place.

Judgements such as beautiful and ugly, admirable and

mediocre are every bit as dependent on the relative as good and evil. How could aestheticism lead to the absolute? Can a work of art take us there? Sometimes, yes – but only if it renounces being its own end or its own objective; only if it tends towards or reveals silence; only if it shows us, as only the greatest do, that the absolute is not an art and matters more than any and all works of art. Beauty is merely a path. Work is merely a path. Where does it lead? To the same place as all paths lead, namely, to that place which contains all paths and is not itself a path. Beauty, as Friedrich von Schelling put it, is 'infinity represented in a finite way'. I would add that it is the absolute represented in a relative way and eternity represented in a temporal way. Such is the quintessence of Mozart and what makes him at once irreplaceable and so profoundly moving: in giving us some of the most beautiful music of all time (musically speaking, we remain in the field of the relative), he enables us to sense that there is something more precious than music, more precious than beauty, something that verges on silence, eternity and peace, something that points – and very nearly leads – to the field of the absolute.

Good and evil, beauty and ugliness, justice and injustice – all these things exist only relatively, through and for humankind. Thus, they do exist. We should no more abolish them than we should absolutize them. Thus, down with nihilism, but down, too, with aestheticism, moralism and politicism – if by the latter three terms we mean the attempt to absolutize art, morals or politics. Does this mean that the absolute is elsewhere? No, just the opposite: it means that the absolute is here, always already here, before all art works, all judgements and all commitments – because it precedes and encompasses them, because it is what allows them to exist and to cease existing. How could music or poetry abolish silence, since they are accompanied by silence, since silence is what they sing and what they depend upon? How could politics or morals abolish the reality that contains them and that they transform? Is another world possible? Definitely – the only impossibility is for the world not to change – but it is not the dream of a militant or a moralist; it is still the world. Only reality is real, and it contains all judgements. How, then, could judgements judge it absolutely?

Relativism and mysticism go hand in hand. Spinoza understood this truth; Prajnanpad confirms it. All morals being relative, how can the absolute be moral? The absolute being amoral, how can morals be anything but relative? The same is true, of course, of beauty and justice. The mistake – and this is where the fate of our modern age is being played out – would be to confuse relativism, which is the truth of politics, art and politics, with nihilism, which is their negation. Given that all values are relative (they depend upon subjects, history, society . . .), it can be said that the absolute has no value. But it can be said only to the extent that we do not inhabit the absolute. When we do inhabit it, it is the very opposite of nothingness. It is being itself, which fulfils and delights us, which, as Spinoza would say, we love: 'Love is joy accompanied by the idea of an outside cause.' Our values can exist only within it. Thus, they do exist. We should not deny them, much less overturn them. This is where Spinoza diverges from Nietzsche, and of course Spinoza is right. Rather, we should say yes to everything, and thus to our judgements as well, but in full awareness of their relativity – and this is what I mean by *acceptance*.

It has nothing to do with optimism, still less with denial or resignation. Etty Hillesum, just a few days before departing to her death at Auschwitz, expressed it admirably:

> People sometimes say to me, 'Oh, yes, you look on the bright side of everything.' What a platitude! Everything is perfectly good, and at the same time perfectly bad . . . I have never felt that I had to force myself to see the bright side of things: everything is always perfectly good, just as it is. Every situation, no matter how deplorable, is an absolute and contains good and evil within itself. By this I simply mean that I find the expression 'seeing the bright side of everything' just as repugnant as 'taking advantage of everything'.

This does not do away with suffering or death. But the suffering and death of Etty Hillesum in no way obliterate what she lived, which she called 'acceptance', 'acquiescence' or 'comprehension', and which is very akin to love.

Independence

Acceptance and liberation go hand in hand, as do freedom and necessity. Such is the spirit of Stoicism, and of Spinozism. Such, too, is the spirit of psychoanalysis, when it has spirit! Such is the spirit of Prajnanpad, who contributed to introducing Freud's doctrines into India. Reality dominates, since it is all there is. What about thought? Either it is reality itself (the truth) or it is merely illusion, which is also part of reality (it is truly illusory). Either it is all, or it is merely a dream of the ego, which is part of the all (it is truly egocentric). What about error? It is truly wrong. And lies? They are truly false. Thus, everything is true. But this truth contains us; we do not contain it. At most we can contain a certain amount of knowledge. This puts ideas in their place. Indeed, what ideas remain, when words vanish? Silence leads to acceptance, which leads to liberation. All of our conditioning is then suspended; so, too, are morals, manners, even simple courtesy. Dogmas, rules, commandments, churches, political parties, opinions, doctrines, ideologies and gurus fall away. All that remains is reality. All that remains is truth. How free we suddenly feel! 'The truth shall make you free', as Saint John's Gospel puts it. This is what we experience at such times, except that the liberation is no longer in the future but in the present, no longer in a book but in the world. Truth obeys no one. That is why it is free, and freeing. And since there is nothing other than truth, it commands no one, either. To what or to whom could it give orders? At such times, we have neither God nor master. This is what I call *independence*, which Swami Prajnanpad says is the true name for spirituality.

It is not the same thing as free will. If everything is real, everything is necessary. How, in the present, could we be different from what we are, want something different from what we want or act differently from the way we act? That freedom, as Spinoza and Freud have shown, is merely ignorance of the causes that weigh upon us, and it prevents us from confronting them.

Nor is it the same thing as fatalism. Only the present exists. How can we be prisoners of the past since it no longer exists? How can the future be predetermined since it does not yet exist? Things are inscribed only within ourselves. This is what Prajnanpad, along with Freud, called the unconscious, namely, the presence of the past within us: 'The only enslavement in life is enslavement to the past [that is, inasmuch as it is present in the unconscious]. People who free themselves of the past are freed. Why? Because the past is the only cause of the future.' Thus, freedom and eternity go hand in hand.

Neither free will nor fatalism: nothing is contingent and nothing is predetermined. All that exists is history, whether individual or collective. All that exists is reality in action, of which my own actions are a part. We should try, not to be other than what we are, but to be what we are *in truth*, and truth has no ego. Again, this is why it is free – because it is universal. Truth, and truth alone, can liberate us from the prison of the self.

'What is perfection?' asks Prajnanpad. And his simple answer is: 'No dependence.' Perfection is to be freed from our childhood, our unconscious, our parents and our milieu. 'To be free,' says the swami elsewhere, 'is to be free from father and mother, nothing else.' It is to be free from self. What remains? Everything. The point is not to heal the ego but to heal ourselves *of* ego; not to save our selves but to break free of them.

All egos are dependent, always. When dependence ends, so does the ego.

To philosophize is to learn detachment: we are not born free; rather, we become that way, and it is a never-ending process. And yet, in the experience I am describing, freedom seems to be suddenly realized and permanently available. This may be because we are prisoners only of our selves – that is, our habits, frustrations, roles, refusals, intellects, ideologies, pasts, fears, hopes, judgements . . . When all this disappears, so do the prison and the prisoner, and all that remains is truth, which has neither subject nor master.

Death and Eternity

I have been trying to express as accurately as possible, and also to comprehend to some extent, certain moments that I have lived, felt or experienced. Far from precluding these moments, my atheism favoured them. Yes, on a few rare occasions, I have had the good fortune of being simply alive, inhabiting reality directly and seeing it face to face, or, rather, seeing it from the inside, not 'as it is', which would be meaningless, but with no mediation other than my body, which is part of reality and in no way an intermediary. At these moments, I have seen reality as it is or as it appears to be. The distinction is irrelevant at such times, for appearances are part of reality. I have been at one with it, with no duality, no problem, no solution, no interpretation – freed from both questions and answers, lacking nothing, no longer cut off from myself and from everything, silent in silence, a passer-by in time's passing (present in the present, changing in the becoming, eternal in eternity!), fearing nothing, hoping for nothing, saying yes to everything (or, rather, not even needing to say it; I *was* that yes), depending on nothing but the universe – and being free, so necessarily and perfectly free that even the question of free will no longer existed.

Such has been my path – or such, at least, have been some of the stopping points and summits along my path. However, they are far too similar to what other people have experienced and described to be contingent on my private history. This is why, though it may cause some to smile, I dare mention such intensely private experiences. In summary, I would say that I, too, have felt and experienced – rarely, but powerfully enough for them to be unforgettable – moments of mystery, self-evidence, plenitude, simplicity, unity, silence, eternity, serenity, acceptance and independence . . . That, at least, is how I perceive and name them, necessarily in retrospect. At the time, I insist, there were no words. There was only an experience, and it was indivisible. Plenitude, simplicity, silence, eternity and so forth – *all of this was one.* It was a sensation – or several inseparable sensations. It was an awareness that had neither words nor subject. It was the very reality I was experiencing and of which I was a part. It was my life – reconciled at long last with itself, and with everything.

Again, I know of no experience as wonderful, as simple, as powerful or as overwhelming as this one. It was like a joy with no commencement (what Spinoza called beatitude, which, being eternal, can begin only fictively), like a peace without end. It has made me no less mortal; in those moments death mattered not at all ('for life in the present,' said Wittgenstein, 'there is no death'), and the memory of them today helps me accept death. Death can deprive me only of my future and my past, which do not exist. The present and eternity (the present, *therefore* eternity) are beyond its reach. It can deprive me only of my self. Thus, it will deprive me of everything and nothing. All truth is eternal, as Spinoza showed. Death will merely deprive me of my illusions.

Mysticism and Atheism

Naturally, the type of experience I have just described proves nothing. All proofs are relative: the absolute is unprovable by definition. Nor does the experience say anything about the existence or nonexistence of God. At these times, the question itself no longer exists. I'm well aware that other people have had other types of 'peak' experiences – an encounter, an ecstasy, a great love . . . It is up to them to describe these things, if they wish and are able to do so. Still, it is probably no coincidence that mystics have so often got into trouble with their churches, when they had churches. Al-Hallāj was burned alive; Meister Eckehart and Fénelon were condemned by the pope . . . These were not mere misunderstandings. The French Jesuit Henri-Marie Cardinal de Lubac said as much in his preface to a voluminous anthology of writings entitled *The Mysticism of Mystics*. A mystic, he wrote, is the very opposite of a prophet: 'The prophet receives and transmits the word of God to which he adheres through faith; the mystic is sensitive to an inner light that exempts him from believing. The two are incompatible.' This is because, as de Lubac said, 'mysticism eats away at myth, and eventually the mystic can do without it; he tosses it away like an empty shell, while remaining indulgent towards those who still need it'. What church or revealed religion could accept this? Father de Lubac went on to quote Emil Brunner: 'It is either the Gospels or contemplation; either mysticism or the Book.' I would add: it is either silence or the Word, either experience or faith, either meditation or prayer.

Far from being an oxymoron, the notion of atheistic mysticism – or, as Father de Lubac put it, mystical atheism

– then becomes self-evident, both as a concept and as a historically observable phenomenon, admittedly more so in the East than in the West. 'In its final state of realization,' our Jesuit priest went on, 'natural mysticism would be naturalistic and verge upon "pure mysticism"; no longer recognizing any object [I would say: any transcendent object], it could be described as the hypostasized mystical intuition: what appears to us as the profoundest form of atheism.' Why not? Leibniz, in a letter written in 1695, had already pointed out that the writings of mystics contained 'extremely bold passages . . . almost verging on atheism'. More radically, Alexandre Kojève in his *Reasoned History of Pagan Philosophy* went so far as to suggest that 'all authentic Mysticisms are in fact more or less atheistic'. Though extreme, the expression says something important, namely (and this takes us back to the beginning of the present chapter), that religion and spirituality are two different things. Even the mystical experience, in which both can culminate, dissuades us from conflating the two.

Nietzsche summed it up famously when he wrote, 'I am a mystic and believe in nothing.' This is not as self-contradictory as it may seem. Mystics are defined by a certain type of experience, comprising self-evidence, plenitude, simplicity, eternity . . . All this leaves very little room for belief.

They see. Why would they need dogma?

Everything is present. Why would they need hope?

They live in eternity. Why would they need to wait for it?

They are already saved. Why would they need a religion?

Whether they are believers or not, mystics are those who no longer lack God. But is a God who is no longer lacking still God?

The Absolute and the Relative

Each person must judge for himself or herself. Personally, I can testify that being an atheist is in no way an obstacle to having, enjoying and rejoicing in a life of the spirit – up to and including the extreme experience in which it silently culminates by vanishing.

When God is no longer lacking, what remains? The plenitude of what is, which is neither a God nor a subject.

When the past and the future no longer separate us from the present, what remains? Eternity – that is, the perpetual *now* of reality and truth.

When ego and intellect no longer separate us from reality, what remains? The silent unity of all.

God, as I said at the outset, is the absolute in act and in person. It goes without saying that I have nothing against those who believe in him. What I experienced at such moments, however, was something very different, something that at the time removed even the longing for God. Whereas God is the all as Other (transcendence), I then inhabited the All itself (immanence). Whereas God is a Subject, no subject remained. Whereas God is the Word, there was only silence. Whereas God is Judge and Saviour, there was no one left to be judged or saved.

We are separated from the absolute, or from eternity, only by our selves. This is what I myself believe. It is what I have experienced on occasion – when the ego vanishes, awareness and body remain, and this is enough to allow the experience to occur – or, rather, this is the experience itself. It is what I have attempted to understand, as a philosopher. It is what, all these years later, I continue to rejoice in. It is what gives me a certain amount of peace.

It is not a consolation. For as long as it remains with us, the ego is inconsolable, and when it is no longer with us, there is no one left to be consoled. It is, however, a form of grace – like the memory, for as long as it lasts, of eternal happiness, or the announcement, despite anxiety and fatigue, suffering and horror, of an already-realized salvation. Hell and heaven are one and the same thing, and that thing is the world. But hell exists only for egos, and heaven only for spirits.

In the long history of spirituality Nagarjuna is the one who, in my opinion, has summed it up best: 'As long as you distinguish between samsara and nirvana,' he wrote, 'you are in samsara.' As long as you distinguish between life as it is – disappointing, exhausting, anxiety-provoking – and salvation, you are in life as it is. As long as you distinguish between eternity and time, you are in time. As long as you distinguish between the absolute and the relative, you are in the relative.

What happens when you stop making these distinctions – or, rather, when they stop making you? You no longer lack God, and the ego no longer weighs you down. You lack nothing, for everything is present, true, eternal and absolute. Prajnanpad: 'To see the relative as relative is to be in the absolute.' Nothing – not even your self – separates you from it.

All that remains is the all, and little does it matter what you call it. All that remains is limitlessness (Anaximander), becoming (Heraclitus), being (Parmenides), Tao (Lao-tzu), nature (Lucretius, Spinoza), the world (what Wittgenstein calls 'the set of everything that occurs'), reality 'without a subject and without end' (Louis Pierre Althusser), the one-without-a-second (Prajnanpad), the present or silence (Krishnamurti) – the absolute in act and without a person.

A Spirituality for Everyday Life

For most of us, such moments remain extremely rare. Some people, it would seem, never experience them. Others, including myself, experience them only on a few occasions. Too few for a whole spiritual life to be based upon them? Perhaps. Enough, however, to give us an idea and a foretaste of such a life, to illuminate it, guide it and become its goal for as long as it needs one, or its criterion. It is something like the vanishing point in a painting or a perspective drawing – the nonrepresented, nonsignified point round which the rest can be organized and take on meaning. The absolute (or eternity, or silence . . .) is that point, for as long as we haven't reached it and remain within the relative, within the painting. This is only a metaphor, though; in reality, the two become as one. This unity is what the mystical experience sometimes seems to achieve – and what, the rest of the time, it is content to aim for. This is already far better than nothing. It is rare and marvellous to experience, at one and the same time, mystery and self-evidence, plenitude and simplicity, unity and eternity, silence and serenity, acceptance and independence . . . Such are the summits of human existence, which can be reached only very exceptionally. We cannot settle into them as if they were armchairs, nor can we manage them as if they were resources or capital. But if we once attain these summits, we realize that we have never left and will never leave them, that absolute and relative, salvation and quest, goal and path are one and the same thing, and that the summit of life is none other than life itself in its true expression, which is to say its eternity. No one, at least in the Western tradition, has expressed this better than Spinoza: 'Beatitude', he wrote, 'is not the price of virtue; it is virtue itself.' Virtue is not a duty but a liberation, not an ideal but a plenitude, not an asceticism but a joy. It is life in action and in truth.

Eastern thinkers have often put it more simply, as in the following well-known haiku:

I am cutting wood
I am drawing water
How marvellous

Only rarely do we inhabit eternity – or, rather, only rarely are we aware that we inhabit it. Almost all of us, on the other hand, have experienced moments of at least partial attention, plenitude, peace, simplicity, freshness, lightness, truth, serenity, presence, acceptance and freedom. Such is the path upon which we find ourselves (the path of spirituality: spirit as path) and along which we can advance.

Those who have followed it to its end, even once, know that it leads nowhere – except, that is, right where we already are. The absolute is not the end of the road (at least, it is that end only as long as we haven't reached it yet); it is the road itself.

In everyday life, of course, such people must continue walking along their paths like everyone else. Spirituality is the walking, but *sub specie temporis*, from the point of view of time, as Spinoza would put it. What the mystical experience affords us, for the space of an instant, is the path itself, but *sub specie aeternatis*, from the point of view of eternity – a spirituality of the everyday, a mysticism of eternity.

'We cannot give the wind orders,' as Krishnamurti put it, 'but we must leave the window open.' The absolute is the wind; our spirit is the window.

Interiority and Transcendence, Immanence and Openness

To put it very simply, we can say that there are two basic ways of conceiving religious spirituality – as an interiority (such is the spirit of Romanesque churches) or as a verticality (such is the spirit of Gothic cathedrals). The two are by no means incompatible; their duality structures religion from within and lends it strength. 'God more deeply within me than I myself,' wrote Saint Augustine, yet higher than the heavens . . .

As time goes by, I find both of these conceptions less and less appealing. I have grown wary, not only of loftiness, which crushes everything, but also of interiority, introspection, the 'I myself'. I find it easier to believe in spiritualities that open on to the world, on to other people, on to everything. Again, to my way of thinking, the goal is not to save the self but to be free of it, not to be locked into our souls but to inhabit the universe. Such is the spirit of Buddha – no Self, neither atman nor Brahman. Such is the spirit of Spinoza – no freedom within me other than the truth, which is all. Such is the spirit, full stop. Open the windows! Open the ego until, as Prajnanpad put it, it becomes 'a circle so huge that it can no longer contain anything, a circle whose radius is infinite – a straight line!' The spirit is itself this openness – yes, 'opening on to Openness', as Rilke said – not the touchy, cramped withdrawal into 'inner life'.

How could I contain the absolute? The absolute contains *me* – I can reach it only by leaving myself behind.

When you come right down to it, this is what phenomenologists call intentionality. 'All awareness', Husserl wrote, 'is awareness of something.' Thus, Sartre agreed, 'awareness has no "inside"; it is nothing but the outside of itself.' Its exact opposite, according to Sartre, is the 'digestive philosophy' of interiority – that philosophy professed by spiritualists who, no matter where they go, perceive only the 'soft and elegant fog of themselves'. 'Thus,' added Sartre in another part of the same text, 'we are freed of "inner life", closed shutters, the damp interiority of gastric life and the sweet cuddling of our souls, since in the final analysis everything up to and including ourselves is outside, in the world, among other people.'

Alain, though he did not mention intentionality and (at least at the time) had not read Husserl, was thinking along much the same lines long before Sartre. In that admirable work of his youth, the *Lorient Notebooks*, for instance (which long remained unpublished), he wrote, 'Thought should have no home apart from the entire universe: only there can it be free and true. Outside ourselves! Outside! Salvation is in the truth and in being.' In other words, salvation is not within my self. Spirituality is the very opposite of introspection. One should not spend one's life gazing at one's navel, one's unconscious or one's soul! As Alain explains, either there is no such thing as an inner life or else it is a bad thing. The inner world is the world of depression and boredom: 'What a sad world that world is. What could be sadder than a self in which being (quite a garrison!) has to take up lodgings? Where am I supposed to lodge all that? More and more keep arriving. The house fills up; the army of pains is inexhaustible. Crowding, stench, nausea. Throw open the windows. More suffering floods in from outside. What is needed, you see, is for the window to swallow up the house – there is room for the universe only in the universe. Enough! I've had enough of my own dream; I want to walk in God's!'

There is no God, however; there is only a dream with no dreamer, or a dream that contains all dreamers. That dream is the world, and we can reach it only by awakening.

Awakening and liberation are the same thing – that is, reaching the universal or the true (the true, *thus* the universal) by being freed of our selves. 'For the awakened,' as Heraclitus put it, 'there is only one world, and they all share it. Sleeping people live each in his own world, and cannot stop fidgeting' – as we do in bed at night or in a dream from which we cannot break free. The self is that dream. The truth is that awakening.

Spiritual life, as I said at the beginning of this chapter, is the life of the spirit – but only, I should have added, inasmuch as we can break free, at least partially and occasionally, from what Kant called our 'precious little selves', our precious little fears, resentments, self-interest, anxieties, worries, frustrations, hopes, compromises and conceits. Is it a matter of 'dying to oneself'? The expression recurs in the writings of many mystics, Christian mystics in particular. Often, however (in Simone Weil, for instance), it puts too much emphasis on the death wish. Rather, I would say that it is a matter of living more – of living at last, rather than hoping to live – and, in order to do so, leaving oneself up behind as much as possible: not dying to oneself, therefore, but opening oneself up to life, to reality, to everything. What could be more boring, more restricted and more vain than my self? Reality is so much more interesting, so much vaster and more variegated! The entire world is there for us to know, understand and love. Humanity is a part of it, and it is there for us to serve, respect and perpetuate. Wise people need no more than this; modestly, they are content with the all.

There are no wise people. All of us, however, have our moments of wisdom, just as all of us have our moments of madness, egoism and pettiness. Only truth can lead us to the former and free us from the latter, and it can free us all the more because it is simple. It has no ego. How could the truth be egotistic? How could the ego be true? To know the self is to dissolve it. Here, the teachings of human sciences and structuralism, as Claude Lévi-Strauss was well aware, converge with the wisdom of sages from time immemorial. The truth of the subject is not a subject. How could a subject be the truth? Wise people have no ego. How could the ego be wise?

The self is neither more nor less than the set of illusions

it has about itself. We can leave it, however – through knowledge, through action – and this is what is known as spirit. 'The wise man knows himself,' as Lao-tzu put it. Thus, he knows he is not wise. All truth is universal. How could a truth belong to me? The universe contains me. How could I contain it, even in thought?

The truth is too huge for me – or, rather, I am too tiny for it. The tininess is what I call the ego. The hugeness is what I call the spirit. Thus, the ego is a slave, and locks us up; the spirit is free, and sets us free.

Mankind, as Pascal said, is at once contemptible and grand. The self is contemptible, I would say, and the spirit is grand. To explain this, there is no need to believe in God or original sin! Nature suffices, and includes culture. Truth suffices, and contains the self, which cannot contain it. The *all* suffices, since there is nothing else. This is a spirituality of immanence rather than transcendence, of openness rather than interiority.

I appreciate Romanesque churches and admire Gothic cathedrals, but I learn far more from humanity, which built them, and from the world, which contains them.

Love and Truth

When I was fifteen or sixteen years old, an idea came to me, perhaps my first personal idea on the subject of God. It was no doubt rather naïve, as first ideas tend to be, but it stayed with me for a long time. The weather that day – a Sunday, as I recall – was rainy and depressing. I was alone, looking out of the window in my bedroom at the top of the house, my forehead pressed against the pane. As I stood there watching the rain fall on the garden, the roof-tops and the surrounding neighbourhood, I was overcome by a sense of lassitude at the meaninglessness of it all. But I had not yet read Ecclesiastes. I merely picked up the notebook I used as a sort of spiritual diary and jotted down the following thought: 'Either God exists, in which case nothing matters, or else God does not exist, in which case nothing matters.'

This left few paths open to me. It is the logic of the absolute, in so far as it is opposed to the relative: everything that is not God is nothingness or lesser being. The world, Plato said, is like a cavern in which we spend our time chasing after shadows. Pascal expressed this beautifully: 'For life is a dream, only slightly less inconstant.' Such is the logic of transcendence. Such is the logic of religion, which, despite its nobility and grandeur, can lead to fanaticism. What does a single human life weigh, in the scales of the absolute?

Transcendence being in keeping neither with my mood at the time nor with the mood of *the* times, I was far more attracted by the other path – which is the same one, really, only going downwards. The logic of immanency, the logic of despair, the logic of nihilism, as Nietzsche so accurately understood it: just *because* all value and all reality have been concentrated in God, what remains when faith vanishes is a world of emptiness and vanity, a world in which everything seems worthless, insipid and irrelevant . . . 'What does nihilism mean?' asked Nietzsche. 'It means that the higher values have depreciated; that the ends have vanished; that there is no longer any answer to the question "What's the use?"' This is the very ebb of living: heart and spirit at low tide. It took me years to emerge from it and rediscover – or, rather, *acquire* – a taste for reality, pleasure and action, the (at least intellectual) transformation of despair into happiness and immanence into wisdom.

Not in vain have I philosophized. Thinking back to that depressing sentence I wrote as a teenager, I see that today I would be tempted to say just the opposite: 'Either God exists, in which case everything matters, or God does not exist, in which case everything matters.' That, however, would be going too far, or, rather, it would be missing the point: things do not matter in and of themselves, but only through the attention we bring to them and the love we bear them. Such is the principle of what, above, I called relativism. 'Not because things are good do we desire them,' wrote Spinoza in substance. 'Rather, we judge them to be good because we desire them.' Such, too, it seems to me, is the principle of charity. We do not love an object because it is valuable; rather, our love confers value upon what we love.

Thus, all values are relative and proportionate to the love we bring to them. Here is where relativism, atheism and fidelity can be seen to converge: love is the supreme value, since there can be value only through love (fidelity); yet what I value is not an absolute, since it is valid only for those who love it (relativism), nor is it a God (atheism).

This sets me at a remove from nihilists at least as much as from believers. The absolute, to my way of thinking, is not God, nor does it love us. This is no reason to stop believing in it, albeit relatively, nor is it a reason to renounce loving.

To quote Pascal a final time, 'Truth without charity is not God.' I agree. This is both what separates us and what brings us together. To believe in God is to believe in an infinitely loving and thus infinitely lovable truth. To be an atheist, on the contrary, is to think that the truth loves neither us nor itself. This is what I call despair. But who said we could love only what loves us in return? Not the Gospels, anyway . . . such is the truth of Calvary. Even a crucified love is preferable to a triumphant hatred.

What brings us together, then, is the space of communion and fidelity. What separates us are metaphysics and religion – and this, too, must be accepted. 'My God, my God, why hast thou forsaken me?' Because he does not exist, the atheist will answer. Because the truth is not God; because it does not love us; because love is not all-powerful; because the only love that truly exists is mortal, incarnate love . . . This is what might be called the tragedy of finitude. It is a part of the human condition, especially for atheists, but it is *only* a part of it. The truly important things are elsewhere – in the love (thus joy) and truth (thus universality) of which we are capable. This is the only wisdom and the only path. What is spirituality? Our finite relationship to infinity or immensity, our temporal experience of eternity, our relative access to the absolute. By all accounts, this leads to joy and – when one comes out on the far side of despair – proves love right. 'To love is to rejoice,' as Aristotle put it. Or Spinoza: 'Love is joy accompanied by the idea of an outside cause.' That truth is unloving by no means condemns love to being untrue, since it is true that we love, nor does it prevent us from loving truth. The joy of knowing, which is ephemeral like all joys and eternal like all truths, is the only path we have to salvation, wisdom and beatitude – but in the here and now. It is the true love of truth.

Here is where all our different themes converge without conflating.

Fidelity to truth: rationalism – the rejection of sophism.

Fidelity to love: humanism – the rejection of nihilism.

Fidelity to a separation between the two: atheism.

Truth is not love; if truth loved itself, it would be God. Rather, love can be true, and it is absolute only in so far as we love truly. Such is the atheists' Pentecost, or the true spirit of atheism: not the Spirit that descends but the spirit that can open us up to the world, other people, to ever-present eternity – and rejoice. The absolute is not love; rather, love can open us up to the absolute.

Thus, ethics can lead to but not replace spirituality, just as spirituality can lead to but not replace ethics. Here, perhaps – at their culmination – is where the wise and the saintly agree:

Love, not hope, is what helps us live. Truth, not faith, is what sets us free.

We are already in the kingdom. Eternity is now.

Acknowledgements

This book owes much to those who encouraged me to write it: Nancy Huston, without whom it would never have existed, Antoine Audouard, Marcel Conche, Susanna Lea, Patrick Renou, Sylvie Thybert, Tzvetan Todorov, Isabelle Vervey and Marc Wetzel. My heartfelt thanks to them. It also owes a great deal to the many debates on these themes in which I have taken part over the years, two of which have been published in France: *A-t-on encore besoin d'une religion?* with Bernard Feillet, Alain Houziaux and Alain Rémond (Editions de l'Atelier, 2003) and *Dieu existe-t-il encore?* with Philippe Capelle (Le Cerf, 2005). My thanks to all of these people for the stimulating exchanges that nourished parts of the book.

Suggested Reading

The following sources, many of them quoted from or alluded to by the author, elucidate themes discussed within the text. Whenever possible, references are to currently available, or at least recently available, editions in English.

Alain (pseudonym of Emile Auguste Chartier). *Alain on Happiness*, trans. Robert D. Cottrell and Jane E. Cottrell. Northwestern University Press, Evanston, Ill., 1989.
———. *Les dieux*, 6me edn. Gallimard, Paris, 1947.
Camus, Albert. *Lyrical and Critical Essays*, trans. Ellen Conroy Kennedy. Vintage, New York, 1970. (Especially the section *The Wrong Side and the Right Side*.)
———. *The Stranger*, trans. Matthew Ward. Vintage, New York, 1946, 1989.
Descartes, René. *Meditations and Other Metaphysical Writings*, trans. Desmond M. Clarke. Penguin, New York, 1999.
Durkheim, Emile. *The Elementary Forms of Religious Life*, trans. Karen E. Fields. The Free Press, Simon & Schuster, New York, 1995.
(Pseudo-)Dionysius the Areopagite. *The Works of Dionysius the Areopagite*, trans. Revd John Parker. James Parker, London, 1897: Available online at http://www.ccel.org/ccel/dionysius/works.html.

Freud, Sigmund. *Civilization and Its Discontents*, trans. James Strachey. Norton, New York, 1961.

———. *The Future of an Illusion*, trans. James Strachey. Norton, New York, 1989.

Hillesum, Etty. *Etty: The Letters and Diaries of Etty Hillesum 1941–1943*, trans. Arnold J. Pomerans. Eerdmans, Grand Rapids, Mich., 2002.

Hulin, Michel. *La mystique sauvage: Aux antipodes de l'esprit*. Presses Universitaires de France, Paris, 1993.

Hume, David. *Dialogues Concerning Natural Religion*, ed. Martin Bell. Penguin, New York, 1990.

———. *A Treatise of Human Nature*, ed. Ernest C. Mossner. Viking, New York, 1986.

Husserl, Edmund. *Cartesian Meditations: An Introduction to Phenomenology*, trans. Dorion Cairns. Springer, New York, 1977.

Jonas, Hans. *Mortality and Morality: A Search for Good After Auschwitz*, ed. Lawrence Vogel. Northwestern University Press, Evanston, Ill., 1996.

Kant, Immanuel. *Critique of Practical Reason*, trans. Mary Gregor. Cambridge University Press, New York, 1997.

———. *Critique of Pure Reason*, trans. Marcus Weigelt and Max Muller. Penguin, New York, 2008.

Kojève, Alexandre, and Laurent Bibard. *L'athéisme*. Gallimard, Paris, 1998.

Kojève, Alexandre. *Essai d'une histoire raisonnée de la philosophie païenne*. Gallimard, Paris, 1997.

Krishnamurti, Jiddu. *Total Freedom: The Essential Krishnamurti*. Harper, San Francisco, Calif., 1996.

Lao-tzu. *Tao Te Ching*, trans. Stephen Mitchell. HarperCollins, New York, 1992.

La Mettrie, Julien Offroy de. *Man a Machine* and *Man a Plant*, trans. Richard A. Watson and Maya Rybalka. Hackett, Indianapolis, Ind., 1994.

Leibniz, Gottfried Wilhelm, Freiherr von. *Monadology and Other Philosophical Essays*, trans. Paul Schrecker and Anne Martin Schrecker. Prentice Hall, Englewood Cliffs, N. J., 1965.

———. *Philosophical Essays*, trans. Roger Ariew and Daniel Garber. Hackett, Indianapolis, 1989. (Especially 'Principles of Nature and Grace'.)

———. *Theodicy: Essays on the Goodness of God, the Freedom of Man and the Origin of Evil*, trans. E. M. Huggard. Open Court, Chicago, Ill., 1985; Hard Press, Lenox, Mass., 2006.

Lucretius. *On the Nature of the Universe*, trans. Ronald E. Latham, rev. edn. Penguin, New York, 1994.

Marcus Aurelius. *Meditations*, trans. Martin Hammond. Penguin, New York, 2006.

Marx, Karl. *The Difference Between the Democritean and Epicurean Philosophy of Nature*, trans. anonymous. Progress Publishers, Moscow, n.d. Available online at http://www.marxists.org/archive/marx/works/1841/dr-theses/index.htm.

Montaigne, Michel de. *The Complete Essays*, trans. M. A. Screech. Penguin, New York, 1993.

Nagarjuna. *The Fundamental Wisdom of the Middle Way: Nagarjuna's Mulamadhyamakakarika*, trans. Jay L. Garfield. Oxford University Press, New York, 1995.

Nietzsche, Friedrich. *Beyond Good and Evil*, trans. R. J. Hollingdale. Penguin, New York, 2003.

———. *The Portable Nietzsche*, trans. Walter Kaufmann. Penguin, New York, 1977. (Especially *Thus Spoke Zarathustra*, *Twilight of the Idols* and *The Antichrist*.)

Pascal, Blaise. *Pensées* [*Thoughts*], trans. A. J. Krailsheimer. Penguin, New York, 1995.

Swami Prajnanpad. *La vérité du bonheur: Lettres à ses disciples*, tom 3. L'Originel/Accarias, Paris, 1990.

Ravier, André, ed. *La mystique et les mystiques*. Desclée de Brouwer, Paris, 1965.

Rosset, Clément. *Joyful Cruelty*, trans. David F. Bell. Oxford University Press, New York, 1993.

Spinoza, Benedict de. *Ethics*, trans. Edwin Curley. Penguin, New York, 2005.

———. *Theological-Political Treatise: Gebhardt Edition*, 2nd edn., trans. Samuel Shirley and Seymour Feldman. Hackett, Indianapolis, Ind., 2001.

Weil, Simone. *Gravity and Grace*, trans. Emma Craufurd. Routledge, New York, 2002.

———. *Waiting for God*, trans. Emma Craufurd. Putnam's, New York, 1951; HarperCollins, New York, 2001.

Wittgenstein, Ludwig. *Tractatus Logico-Philosophicus*, rev. edn. Routledge, New York, 1974, 2001.